PUB STROLLS IN
LINCOLNSHIRE

Brett Collier

COUNTRYSIDE BOOKS
NEWBURY BERKSHIRE

First published 2001
© Brett Collier 2001

COUNTRYSIDE BOOKS
3 Catherine Road
Newbury, Berkshire

To view our complete range of books,
please visit us at
www.countrysidebooks.co.uk

ISBN 1 85306 675 3

*To Janet, the best of companions
on the longest journey of all since
we met on that mountain in Kenya*

Photographs by the author
Maps by the author and redrawn by Techniset Typesetters
Designed by Graham Whiteman

Typeset by Techniset Typesetters, Newton-le-Willows
Produced through MRM Associates Ltd., Reading
Printed in Italy

Contents

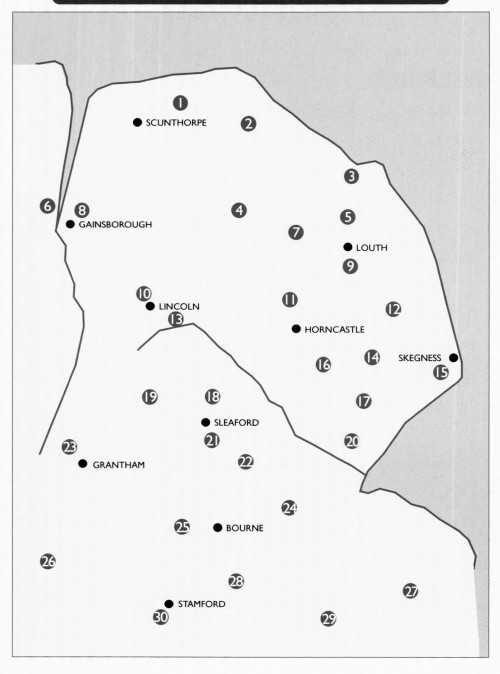

PUBLISHER'S NOTE

We hope that you obtain considerable enjoyment from this book; great care has been taken in its preparation. However, changes of landlord and actual closures are sadly not uncommon. Likewise, although at the time of publication all routes followed public rights of way or permitted paths, diversion orders can be made and permissions withdrawn.

We cannot, of course, be held responsible for such diversion orders and any inaccuracies in the text which result from these or any other changes to the routes nor any damage which might result from walkers trespassing on private property. We are anxious though that all details covering the walks and the pubs are kept up to date and would therefore welcome information from readers which would be relevant to future editions.

The sketch maps accompanying each walk are not always to scale and are intended to guide you to the starting point and give a simple but accurate idea of the route to be taken. For those who like the benefit of detailed maps, we recommend that you arm yourself with the relevant Ordnance Survey map in the Explorer series.

Lincolnshire is blessed with a variety of landscapes from the Wolds, to the Marsh, the Heath and the Fen, and it is certainly not flat. The locations of these walks were selected to give a good geographical spread, to provide a variety of landscapes and in some cases to suggest places that were likely to be unknown to many people who may have lived in the area for some years. How often have you looked out of the car window when driving and thought that an area of countryside looked lovely but have never had a reason to stop and explore? This book provides such an opportunity, with 30 walks ranging in length from $1^3/_4$ to 5 miles that take full advantage of Lincolnshire's wonderful views and wide skies.

Another consideration for selection was that a reasonably easy walk was available in the immediate vicinity of a good inn (which is why one walk takes you just over the county border to West Stockwith). Inns today are as much restaurants as a venue for drinking. All those chosen serve food – often surprisingly good value and sometimes unusual, interesting meals.

Most landlords are happy about your leaving a vehicle in their car park but it is courteous to leave a note stating that you intend to return and become a customer. Nowadays, an unattended car out of normal hours may cause some concern and leaving a note not only establishes a contact but invariably means a warm greeting upon your return.

Sketch maps are provided for each walk with numbered points that correspond to the numbered paragraphs in the walk directions, but the ability to read and use an Ordnance Survey map to check various features will greatly enhance one's enjoyment of the countryside and therefore the relevant OS Explorer sheet is noted.

Countryside Officers cannot be everywhere and they welcome reports from walkers regarding public rights of way that have not been properly reinstated after ploughing, are crop obstructed or where there has been a failure to define to the minimum width as the law requires. Please inform The Director, Highways and Planning Directorate, Lincolnshire County Council, City Hall, Lincoln LN1 1DN giving a map reference if possible should you encounter any fieldpath problems en route.

Please respect the life of the countryside and try to obey the Country Code whenever it is possible to do so, particularly about opening or closing gates. It is sensible to leave any gate as you find it. Do attempt to keep to the correct line of any public right of way for detouring around a field edge only leads to confusion for other walkers and may leave you open to the charge that you were nowhere near any public right of way. Most walkers are welcome in the countryside and villagers often remark that it is good to see people using their paths. However, farmers do worry about dogs harming their livestock particularly in the lambing season so please keep dogs under close control.

Even in lowland Lincolnshire it is important to be reasonably shod. No crowded or feet-eroded paths here, though, for one of the attractions of walking in Lincolnshire is that it is still possible to walk on public rights of way and meet hardly anyone, except perhaps in the villages. Do enjoy your strolls from Lincolnshire pubs as much as I have in selecting them.

Brett Collier

Barnetby le Wold
The Railway Inn

MAP REF: OS EXPLORER 281 (GR 055101)

WALK 1

DISTANCE: $2\frac{1}{2}$ MILES

DIRECTIONS TO START: FROM THE M180 JUNCTION WITH THE A15(T) AND THE A180(T) PROCEED DOWNHILL INTO BARNETBY VILLAGE. THE RAILWAY INN IS ON THE LEFT BEFORE YOU REACH THE RAILWAY BRIDGE. **PARKING:** THERE IS AMPLE SPACE IN THE PUB CAR PARK.

Barnetby le Wold is on the very edge of the Wolds, and this walk takes you above the village, with extensive views towards the Humber from the road above Knab's Hill by the strategically sited mill. A large village with a network of narrow lanes and recently developed small estates, Barnetby has railway connections even today and, wonder of wonders in rural Lincolnshire, not only a working railway but also a passenger station. Barnetby has two churches, the newish one in the village and an occasionally used ancient church in a fold on a hillside just beyond the present day settlement.

The Railway Inn

Snug and clean, this is a friendly village pub popular with train spotters and locals. It has railway memorabilia and drawings decorating the walls, including a Porthcawl railway station sign and a Pass of Glencoe poster. Carefully done and kindly served bar food includes a Jumbo Pasty or a Belly Buster including rump steak, gammon and lamb plus liver, kidney and sausages. John Smith's Cask Beer, Tetley's, Worthington Bitter and an Extra Smooth are served plus two lagers, Carling Black Label and Foster's. The pub is open Monday to Friday 2 pm to 11 pm, Saturday 12 noon to 4 pm and 7 pm to 11 pm. On Sunday they are open from 12 to 4 pm and 7 pm to 10.30 pm. The kitchen closes at 9 pm each evening. There are ample car parking areas, a beer garden and a children's play area. Telephone: 01652 688284.

PLACES OF INTEREST NEARBY

Elsham Hall Country and Wildlife Park, near Brigg, has lakeside gardens, a wild butterfly garden, an adventure playground, and a carp feeding jetty. Opening times 11 am to 5 pm from Easter Sunday to mid-September. Telephone: 01652 688698.

The **Humber Bridge** has a viewing area, free parking, toilets and a picnic area. It is well signed through Barton on Humber. The bridge was, before the Ma Wan Channel Bridge in Hong Kong, the longest single span bridge in the world. There is an exhilarating walk over the bridge and a bus service.

The Walk

① Turn left from the car park along the upper road and then down the steps at the end and cross the road onto the footway. Immediately after going under the bridge, recross the road to follow the signposted footpath on a clear track with the railway on your left.

② On reaching the stile on the right at the top of Knab's Hill, cross the rough pasture aiming slightly to the right of the bridge. Go through the kissing gate and climb the bridge embankment to the lane. Turn right along the lane, passing the designated motor bike scrambling quarry on the right and enjoying far reaching views towards the Humber. Pass the attractive green lane signposted as a bridleway, and 300 yards beyond the mill turn right off the lane onto a signposted footpath.

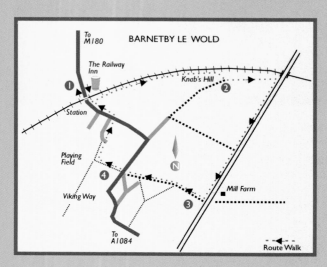

Down 'the cliff' to the village

③ Follow this footpath first as a field-edge path across the hilltop and then when you cross into the next field follow the line of electricity posts down towards the houses where you will find a stile. Go down the narrow, rather muddy lane to the road.

④ Go directly across the road up the track and through the wooden fieldgate or the pedestrian gap. Turn right on reaching Low Farm with the village playing field directly in front. On reaching the small housing estate follow the road round to the left to the main road. Turn left at the main road and retrace your steps below the railway bridge and up the steps to the top road and the inn.

Keelby
The Nag's Head

| MAP REF: OS EXPLORER 284 (GR 163101) | WALK 2 | DISTANCE: 5 MILES |

DIRECTIONS TO START: TURN OFF THE A18(T) BRIGG TO GRIMSBY ROAD FOR KEELBY,
11½ MILES FROM BRIGG. THE NAG'S HEAD IS SITUATED IN MANOR STREET.
PARKING: THE PUB HAS A LARGE CAR PARK WHERE WALKERS/CUSTOMERS MAY LEAVE THEIR CARS.

Keelby seems to have three 'centres', including that around the village shops. The second is the neatly kept village green overlooked by the modern school buildings and an elegant Gothic war memorial. The memorial has an unusual entry, for on 7th May 1915 Annie and Dorothy Lancaster from the nearby Manor House were drowned in the Atlantic when a German submarine torpedoed the liner *Lusitania*. The third 'centre' is around the church of St Bartholomew and includes some attractive ironstone cottages and the imposing church institute with a clock tower built in 1898. Methodism has always been strong in this area of Lincolnshire and according to the Religious Census of 1851 the Wesleyans numbered 240 at evening worship, with another 70 at the Primitive Chapel and only 34 at the parish church. Beginning past the Methodist chapel and returning past the parish church, this relaxing walk takes you out into the surrounding countryside, through woods and fields and beside a wandering stream.

The Nag's Head

The Nag's Head in Manor Street is near the village green and it is a pleasant pub under new ownership, serving excellently presented and well prepared simple meals. The genuine village atmosphere of this well-run free house with locals playing dominoes, envelops visitors as well as regulars. Bar food includes sandwiches or large filled rolls and a good range of hot dishes changing with the seasons and shown on a daily blackboard. Opening hours are Monday to Saturday 11 am to 11 pm and on Sunday 11 am to 10.30 pm. Beer on offer includes Worthington Draught Dark Mild, John Smith's Extra Smooth and Cask, Stones Bitter and Caffrey's Pale Ale. Lagers are Carling Black Label, Kronenbourg and Miller Pilsner, with Guinness on draught and Scrumpy Jack cider. Meals are served from 12 noon to 2 pm from Tuesday to Saturday and from 12 noon to 3 pm on Sunday. Evening meals are served from 6 pm to 9 pm on Thursday, Friday, Saturday and Sunday. There is a garden area with picnic tables, and a No Smoking area. Dogs are only permitted in the garden. Telephone: 01469 560660.

The Walk

① Turn left out of the pub car park to the village green. Go straight across the green to turn right along Yarborough Road for 200 yards, and by the Methodist chapel turn left down the narrow Roxton Avenue. Go through the fieldgate at the end of the avenue (signpost) and walk along the clear path across the field towards the industrial buildings. Cross the small stream and bear right towards the prominent house, a two-step stile and a signpost onto the track. Go over the accommodation track and continue on the same line to a hedge and gate, aiming to the left of the house. Go over the small triangular field to a two-step stile, a signpost and the lane.

② Turn left along the lane and follow the road around the bend with the wood at first only on the left and later on both sides. Then at the sharp left-hand bend in the lane turn right off the road onto a good track with the wood on your right at first and then open fields.

③ Turn left along the road past Greenlands Farm on the left and later Wood View on the right. Turn right off the road onto a signposted path after you have passed Wood View. There is a hedge on the immediate right of the path. Continue down to the footbridge.

④ Cross the bridge and turn right with the stream on your right and follow the

PLACES OF INTEREST NEARBY

Deep in the prison cells of **Grimsby Town Hall**, pay a visit that will take you on a time travel journey to uncover the town's colourful past. Telephone: 01472 323345. Also in Grimsby is the **National Fishing Heritage Centre**, telephone for details: 01472 342422. Discover what it was like to sail in the Arctic on a deep sea trawler.

Pelham's Pillar can be seen at point 4 of the walk. It is 128 feet tall and was erected in 1849 to commemorate the planting of twelve and a half million trees by the 1st Earl of Yarborough of Brocklesby Park.

A converted chapel at Keelby

track turn left with the hedge on your right until you reach another track crossing your route. Turn right here for a few yards only then left again to proceed in the same direction and continue forward at the end of the hedgeline to a footbridge.

⑤ Cross the bridge and walk forward aiming for the right-hand end of the last bungalow. Follow the track, becoming a road, to the church. Cross over the road to turn right at Manor Street and back to your starting place.

wandering of the stream until you reach a footbridge with another public right of way coming in from the left. Cross the ditchboard and continue left with the stream now on your left. Walk below the electricity wires to turn right on meeting the field boundary away from the stream with Newstead Farm on the right. On meeting the good farm

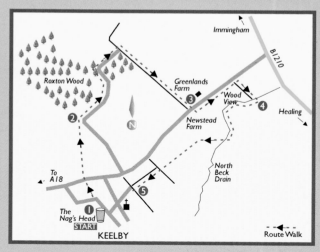

Weelsby
The Hainton

MAP REF: OS EXPLORER 284 (GR 278080)	WALK 3	DISTANCE: 4½ MILES

DIRECTIONS TO START: FROM THE A46 LINCOLN-GRIMSBY ROAD ON APPROACHING NUN'S CORNER IN GRIMSBY WITH THE COLLEGE OVER ON THE LEFT, GET INTO THE RIGHT-HAND LANE MARKED CLEETHORPES. THE HAINTON IS ON THE RIGHT OF THIS ROAD AFTER ¾ MILE. CROSS THE PEAK PARKWAY TRAFFIC LIGHTS (THE OLD RAILWAY) AND ONLY YARDS FURTHER ON TURN RIGHT AT THE NEXT SET OF TRAFFIC LIGHTS INTO PEAKS LANE. THE ENTRY INTO THE CAR PARK FOR THE HAINTON IS ON THE LEFT. **PARKING:** IN THE PUB CAR PARK.

Weelsby nowadays has lost its separate identity and become a suburb of Grimsby, but nevertheless an attractive one on the edge of the countryside. Happily Grimsby is back in Lincolnshire once more and is now the administrative capital of North-East Lincolnshire. Once it was world-renowned as the principal fishing port of the kingdom but the industry has sadly declined.

Although a workaday place today, there are still oases of green reaching into suburbia. The People's Park just to the north of the A46 after you turn at Nun's Corner was given to the town by Lord Heneage in 1883. You will discover on this walk that Weelsby Woods is yet another green oasis for the town, as you weave a path on good tracks around the old railway route.

The Hainton

The Hainton is a Bass house and a rather elegant one. Indeed, the lounge reminds one of the transatlantic liners of the Thirties, or at least how I imagine they were designed and furnished. The bar parlour is rather different with its games annexe. Food is served from 12 noon to 2 pm and from 5.30 pm to 9 pm from Monday to Saturday and 12 to 9 pm on Sunday. Bar meals are good value, including ham and eggs, fish and chips, BBQ Chicken Melt, a double breast of chicken coated with sauce and topped by bacon and melted cheese, or the Ultimate Pie, filled with meat and vegetables and topped with a pastry lid. Snacks include roast meat sandwiches and there is a range of desserts including sticky toffee pudding. Tea and coffee are also served. The Hainton is open from 11 am to 11 pm from Monday to Saturday and from 12 noon to 10.30 pm on Sunday. Stones Bitter, Bass Mild, Worthington, Grolsch, Carling Black Label plus two stouts, Murphy's and Caffrey's are on offer. The licensee has been here several years, loves the trade and, as always, management influences the whole atmosphere and the service offered. Telephone: 01472 341767.

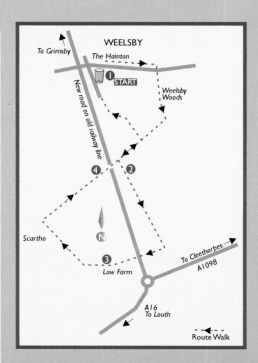

walk up the main drive with the car park on the right. Keep straight forward and at the top of the hill turn right on a signposted path and follow this path round the field edge and eventually onto a track. Walk straight forward on the track towards the Peak Parkway.

② Upon reaching the bridge over the main road turn left on a good track for about 1,000 yards ignoring any tracks to the left. Peaks Tunnel Farm must have once stood at the first track junction but

The Walk

① Walk across the car park at the front of the pub to the right-hand corner where there is a pedestrian exit. Turn right on Weelsby Road for 650 yards. Turn right at Weelsby Wood entrance by the lions and

PLACES OF INTEREST NEARBY

Freshney Bog Nature Reserve at Little Coates is another 'green oasis' for Grimsby. This 35 acre section of the River Freshney, largely enclosed by urban growth, is being developed as a conservation project.

Weelsby Wood

there is little trace of it today. Carr Plantation is over on the left. Turn right on a signposted path by the dyke to a kissing gate onto the Peak Parkway. Cross this fast road with care to the kissing gate opposite and walk on towards Low Farm with its high mast.

③ Turn right around the farm buildings and continue forward on the good, motorable track for $^1/_2$ mile with houses later on the left. Turn right on the clear signposted path back towards the main

road and the splendid new concrete road bridge.

④ Go over the bridge and up the track you walked earlier but turn left on the clear track and still keep left round the bend. Walk straight forward into Peaks Lane with the imposing YMCA building on the left. The track has been blocked at the exit with a tree trunk, presumably to discourage travellers using the lane. The Hainton car park is on the right at the top of the road.

Nettleton
The Salutation Inn

MAP REF: OS EXPLORER 282 (GR 109002)	WALK 4	DISTANCE: 3½ MILES

DIRECTIONS TO START: THE INN IS SITUATED ON THE A46 LINCOLN TO GRIMSBY ROAD AT THE BOTTOM OF CAISTOR BROW. IT IS 7 MILES NORTH OF MARKET RASEN. **PARKING:** PARK OFF THE MAIN ROAD UP COOK'S LANE, DIRECTLY OPPOSITE THE INN. DISCUSSIONS ARE TAKING PLACE REGARDING A PARKING AREA FOR VIKING WAY WALKERS FURTHER ALONG THE VILLAGE.

This is a 'town and country' walk in an area of Outstanding Natural Beauty. One of the finest stretches of the Viking Way long distance recreational path from Barton on Humber to Oakham in Rutland goes through Caistor and up Nettleton Valley, with some of the route from Caistor being used during the walk. The walk starts at Nettleton, rather than Caistor, simply because I consider that the Salutation Inn is the best inn for some miles around.

Caistor was a hill fort of the early Britons, later made into a major Roman camp encircled with a massive wall of which fragments still remain. After the departure of the Romans, Caistor retained its importance and mounds in the area are supposed to mark the site of King Egbert's victory over the Mercians in AD 829. The present day church was in the heart of the Roman citadel and a Roman well, seen during the walk, is still in use today.

The Salutation Inn

There is always a warm and friendly welcome in this civilised Whitbread Pub Partnership country inn, with good, fresh bar snacks and well-kept Landlord, Speckled Hen, Fuller's London Pride, Bass, Whitbread Trophy, Tom Wood and Boddington's bitter on offer plus Stella Artois and Heineken lager and chilled wine on tap. Food is available from 12 noon to 2 pm and then 7 pm to 9.45 pm. The menu changes with the seasons and always has a variety of specials, and a wide range of bar snacks to suit everyone's palate and pocket. The inn is open from 12 noon to 3.30 pm Monday to Saturday and 6 pm to 11 pm throughout the week. On Sunday the pub opens from 12 noon to 3 pm and 7 pm to 10.30 pm. There is a No Smoking area, and a beer garden. Dogs are not permitted. Telephone: 01472 851228.

The Walk

① Heading away from the Salutation Inn, walk up Cook's Lane directly opposite. At

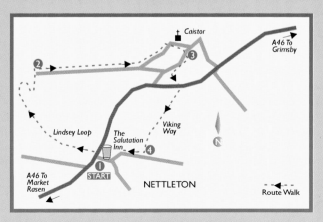

PLACES OF INTEREST NEARBY

Nettleton Wood (Woodland Trust) covers 25 acres and is a short walk from the A46, lying just below the edge of the Wolds with areas of heath and grassland (GR 095995).

Nettleton Top Pasture is a Countryside Agency Access Site with fine views (GR 112993). An interesting example of wet, acid grassland which is being sympathetically managed for the benefit of wildlife without the use of artificial fertilisers or agricultural sprays. Accessible initially until 30th September 2002.

the end of the lane with farm buildings on the left, proceed forward to the stile. Walk straight forward across the paddock towards the right-hand corner of the wire enclosure of the pumping station. Cross the stile by the pumping station and follow the stream on the right. Cross over the stream by the waymarked footbridge to turn left. Follow the stream, now on your left and continue over a stile onto a fine green lane. Go straight on then bear left with the lane avoiding any hedge gaps on the right. Turn right at the stile by the fence just before the Scots pine tree and follow the edge of the field round with the flowing stream on your right. This cross-field path has been diverted around the edge of the field.

② Turn right up the unsurfaced green lane with a dyke on the left. This track becomes Navigation Lane which is rapidly changing its character due to building development. There are still school playing fields on the left. Turn left down

The Roman well at Caistor

primary school and left up the signposted tarmac footpath just beyond Redhill Close. Follow this footpath into Westwold Road, turn left at the T-junction and left again in front of the maisonettes, to pick up the path to the rear of the council houses with the primary school playing field on the left. This path takes you to the A46 road. Cross the road with care and proceed down the steep embankment on a signposted concrete path to a stile. Cross the pasture field keeping to the hedge line on the left and pass through the wide gap at the field corner to the field beyond. Make for the far field corner and cross the stile to keep the hedge now on your right. Cross the next stile and keep the broken hedge/tree line on your immediate right until you reach the double stile in the field corner. Cross this and still keep to the hedge/fence line on the right. Go over the next stile and proceed diagonally right downhill with a bungalow on the right. There is a stile in the right-hand field corner.

Millfields and just beyond Windsor Drive go right through the small recreation area with the brook on your left and follow the path in between the houses. Turn right upon reaching the road and continue uphill for about 130 yards and then right again opposite the post box to walk up a steep minor road with the High School buildings on the left. At the top of the hill turn right by the church wall.

③ Turn left along the graveyard path of St Peter and St Paul's church. Walk down the steps in the corner and look at the spring on the left at the bottom. Turn left up the appropriately named Fountain Street and right at the top down Horsemarket following the rise in the roadside footway on the left. Turn right upon reaching South Dale Road by the

④ Cross the stile and turn right down Mangate Hill for a few yards and then right again along Nettleton village street with the church on your right and continue until you reach the crossroads and the Salutation Inn.

Marshchapel
The White Horse

MAP REF: OS EXPLORER 283 (GR 359993)	**WALK 5**	DISTANCE: $3\frac{1}{2}$ MILES

DIRECTIONS TO START: MARSHCHAPEL IS ON THE A1031 GRIMSBY TO MABLETHORPE ROAD, 12 MILES FROM GRIMSBY. **PARKING:** IN THE PUB CAR PARK.

Marshchapel has one of the finest churches of the Lincolnshire Marsh. The church of St Mary is a magnificent building of Ancaster stone and was completed before 1420 when the bells were hung. The stone used to build the church came from Ancaster to Grainthorpe Haven for at that time Marshchapel was still in a tide-affected marshland. It was originally a chapel belonging to Fulstow but today that village is further inland and smaller than the present day village of Marshchapel. The tide was put to good use by the salt industry for the saltpans of Marshchapel have been frequently mentioned from the Domesday Book onward. Later wealth was created by the draining of the land to make sheep pastures. In the middle of the 19th century some 600 acres of salt 'fitties' (the outmarsh between the sea banks and the sea) were reclaimed. Between the sea and the canal, this is a fascinating walk beneath wide, open skies.

The White Horse

The White Horse is an Enterprise Group pub, well worth visiting just to look at the hundreds of miniature model cars, vans, buses and lorries in display cases around the walls. However, in addition, it is a comfortable village local with a genuine open fire. Bass, Stones, John Smith's, Boddington's and Theakstone's beer is on offer plus Carling Black Label and Kronenbourg lager and Woodpecker and Strongbow cider. Drinks are served from 11.30 am to 3 pm and 7 pm to 11 pm Monday to Saturday with Sunday opening being 12 noon to 3 pm and 7 pm to 11 pm. Meals are served daily from 12 noon to 2 pm and 7 pm to 9.30 pm throughout the week, except Monday evening. It is wise to book in advance for the incredible value of the Sunday lunch. Bar meals offer starters and a wide choice of main courses, including vegetarian dishes, plus sweet courses such as banana split, apple pie, jam roly-poly and treacle sponge. There is a separate dining section, a games room, a picnic area and an adjacent properly equipped children's play area. Only guide dogs are permitted on the premises. Telephone: 01472 388280.

The Walk

① Turn left out of the pub car park along Sea Dyke Road for about 180 yards. Go left at Littlefield Lane with the village post office over on the right. Continue straight forward by Honeysuckle Cottage onto an unsurfaced lane.

This was a smugglers' area in the past, for the flat coast between Mablethorpe and the Humber was ideal for landing cargoes, mainly from Holland, and moving them swiftly inland. So remote was the region that contraband was often moved in daylight using farm waggons but hidden under a load of potatoes or turnips. One smuggled cargo captured off this coast consisted of gin, tea, tobacco and playing cards. Playing cards carried a high duty at that time of two shillings and sixpence per pack and were well worth smuggling.

② Turn left upon reaching the surfaced lane around considerable bends for 700 yards. Turn right up the straight, stoned-track by the electricity post on the immediate right of the track. Continue down this track until you reach Fulstow Bridge footbridge over the Louth Navigation Canal.

The canal was hand-completed by navvies in 1770, only five years after the work began. It was built wide enough to allow two Humber keel boats to pass, importing coal, fruit and vegetables and exporting corn and wool.

③ Turn left along the canal bank with the canal on your right for 900 yards until you reach the lane. Go left up the lane back towards Marshchapel village. At the crossroads go straight ahead.

④ Some 450 yards beyond the crossroads

PLACES OF INTEREST NEARBY

Tetney Lock is the end of the Louth Navigation Canal and there is a seaward walk towards Tetney Haven (GR 344023).

Covenham Reservoir is nearby, with bird life and water sports (GR 340961). Parking.

Along the way

and immediately after the small roadbridge over a stream, turn left on an unsurfaced track marked 'Byway'. Shortly after passing the public footpath with ditchboard crossing the byway it becomes a surfaced lane with some houses. On reaching the village playing field on the right, turn right off the lane to walk down the side of the sports field to discover that you are at the rear of the White Horse.

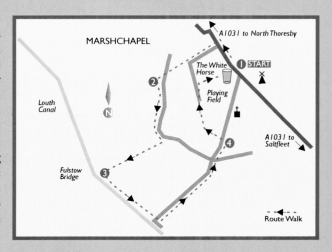

West Stockwith
The Waterfront Inn

MAP REF: OS EXPLORER 280
(GR 785946)

WALK 6

DISTANCE: 2$\frac{1}{2}$ MILES

DIRECTIONS TO START: TURN OFF THE A161 BECKINGHAM-HAXEY ROAD TOWARDS THE RIVER TRENT AT MISTERTON ONTO A MINOR ROAD SIGNPOSTED WEST STOCKWITH. THE INN IS ON THE LEFT JUST OVER THE CANAL BRIDGE. **PARKING:** IN THE PUB CAR PARK.

Those of you who are good at map reading will already have realised something about this particular walk. North Lincolnshire is really a few miles up the road in the Isle of Axholme but this seemed such an excellent pub and a splendid walk that it was a pity not to use West Stockwith, despite the fact that it is not actually in the county. This is a waterside walk *par excellence* with the Chesterfield Canal towpath and the pleasure craft along the canal, interesting lock gates, a quiet cul-de-sac lane with remnants of a former industrial era, the banks of the River Idle and then along the River Trent to a busy marina overlooked by our selected hostelry by Basin Bridge. My companion suggested that it looked like a film set scene. West Stockwith is Nottinghamshire's most northerly outpost and a small place of considerable charm. It is only a couple of hundred yards from East Stockwith in Lincolnshire but unfortunately nowadays there isn't a ferry service across the river.

The Waterfront Inn

The Waterfront Inn is aptly named and the raised patio outside at the front enables visitors to sit at picnic tables and overlook the colourful scene of activities in the marina basin. It is a friendly place with caring licensees who often cater for disabled visitors. It is a free house, offering six real ales, John Smith's and five guest beers plus three ciders, Thatchers, Stowford Press and Scrumpy Jack, two lagers, draught Guinness and ten wines. Opening hours are from Monday to Saturday from 12 noon to 11 pm and on Sunday from 12 noon to 10.30 pm. Meals are served throughout the week from 12 noon to 2.30 pm and in the evening from 6 pm to 8.30 pm. Bar meals on offer include ploughman's, sandwiches, toasties and more substantial meals such as starters of home-made soup and a crusty roll, with main courses such as steak and kidney pie, ham and eggs, battered haddock or gammon steak plus desserts of spotted dick, treacle sponge and a whole host more. Accommodation is available and there is an adjoining caravan park. Telephone: 01427 891223.

The Walk

① Turn right out of the car park and right again down the towpath of the Chesterfield Canal along the recreational path known as the Cuckoo Way. Continue under the railway bridge, past the inn on the right and then under the road bridge to have a look at Misterton Top Lock.

② Take the footpath off the towpath by turning right over the stile just beyond Lock Cottage. Cross the main road to go down the short Station Road by the Victorian postbox set in the wall, to turn left along Soss Lane at the T-junction. Go under the railway and follow the lane round to the left. Actually there is a public footpath behind the hedge but Soss Lane is a cul-de-sac with very little traffic.

③ On reaching the gaunt industrial pump house buildings on the right, cross the footbridge over the Mother Drain and turn right with the River Idle now on your immediate left. Keep along the bank of the river around the large bend past the new extensive waterworks on the left. The path eventually becomes a short road leading into the main street.

④ Go straight across the road and over the concrete balustrade to turn right along the Trent bank back to the marina. Cross over the lock gates and turn right with the administration buildings and the yacht club on the right. Climb the embankment steps at Basin Bridge and the Waterfront Inn is directly across the road.

The River Idle, the Mother Drain and the Chesterfield Canal all join the Trent here and in the 17th and 18th centuries West Stockwith became quite an important inland port with warehouses and boat building yards. Gainsborough

The River Idle

eventually took over much of the trade. Nowadays it is a little faded but the canal basin is still full of boats although almost entirely pleasure craft. The village street runs parallel to the Trent with a small red brick Georgian church on the river bank. Built in 1772 by the executors of William Huntington, 'ship carpenter', the interior is prettily adorned with elegant plaster and woodwork. William Huntington's figure reclines upon his tomb holding in his hands the design of a sailing ship – perhaps one of the sea-going ships he built in his yard here.

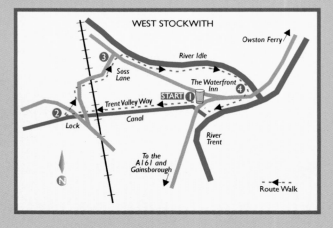

Binbrook
The Plough

| **MAP REF:** OS EXPLORER 282 (GR 211937) | **WALK 7** | **DISTANCE:** 2½ MILES |

DIRECTIONS TO START: TAKE THE B1203 MARKET RASEN-TEALBY-WALTHAM ROAD.
BINBROOK IS 8 MILES FROM MARKET RASEN. **PARKING:** CARS MAY BE LEFT IN THE
PUB CAR PARK IF YOU INTEND TO BE A CUSTOMER UPON YOUR RETURN.
ALTERNATIVELY, ROADSIDE PARKING AT THE SIDE OF THE MARKET SQUARE.

This is a large village on the north-eastern edge of the Lincolnshire Wolds, old enough to be entered in the Domesday Book as Binnibroc. The water mill that you pass on the walk ground corn for local use for many years by means of a turbine. Later, in the 1950s, the turbine was still working but to provide electricity for the occupants of Mill House.

In 1749 a severe fire destroyed many of Binbrook's houses and after the fire rebuilding was done with pantiles. The 1780 manor house is in the market place near the start of the walk. At the head of the Market Place the former Primitive Methodist chapel is now the butcher's shop. In days past there were the usual village craftsmen and Binbrook was famous for its wheelwrights. One of them, George Smith, whose spindle-shaped farm waggons had a great reputation, employed nine men. This is a lovely walk with much of interest to see, including reminders of Binbrook's Air Force connection.

The Plough

The Plough belongs to Clarinbridge, selling John Smith's real ales, Scrumpy Jack cider, draught Guinness and Carling Black Label lager. Chilled house wine is also on offer. The carpeted lounge bar is small but comfortable with lots of local photographs. The large public bar has a games annexe. There is a beer garden and a car park off Back Lane. The pub offers a varied, reasonably priced, traditional bar menu of hot and cold food. It is open for meals from 12 noon to 3 pm and 4 pm to 9 pm Monday to Friday, 12 noon to 4 pm and 5 pm to 9 pm on Saturday and Sunday. Opening hours are from 11 am to 11 pm Monday to Saturday and on Sunday 12 noon to 10.30 pm. Well behaved dogs are allowed in the pub. Telephone: 01472 398241.

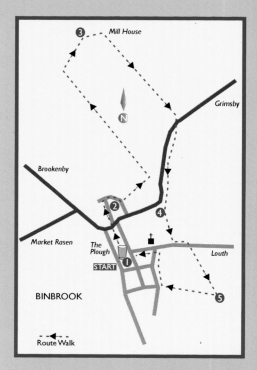

The Walk

① Turn left out of the pub car park into the Market Square with the Manor House on the right. Cross the main road to turn left up the village side lane with the seat marked 'Binbrook' on the grass verge on the left. Turn right down North Halls.

Binbrook is a member of the Countryside Agency Parish Paths Partnership Scheme (3P's) which means that local volunteers help to maintain their public rights of way.

② Turn left off the lane along a public footpath with signpost. The path has recently been diverted out of the nursery and now follows the left-hand boundary down to a footbridge. Cross the bridge and then a few yards of arable field to the track. Turn left down this good stoned track and where it turns right cross the stream and the stile by the bridge. Walking along the bank follow the stream on your right along the attractive path to the old watermill.

PLACES OF INTEREST NEARBY

Willingham Woods has colour-coded forestry walks. Leaflets, parking and toilets available. Find the woods on the A631 road near Market Rasen (GR 138885).

Tealby lies in an Area of Outstanding Natural Beauty and is a winner of the Lincolnshire Best Kept Village Award. A delightful place to explore, with Tennyson connections (GR 157908).

Near Binbrook

③ At the mill turn left down the bank, cross the footbridge and climb the slope with the Mill House now on your right. Follow the good stoned track back down to the main road. At the road turn right downhill towards the village.

④ On reaching Binbrook Motors garage turn left off the road onto a signposted footpath. There are two public footpaths here and you take the left one. Upon reaching the road turn left for a few yards and cross the road to leave the lane and follow the signposted track uphill.

⑤ After 300 yards turn right down the field edge on a signposted path to go down the wooden steps at a steep embankment and then cross a small paddock to a ditchboard and stile.

There is a narrow walkway between houses and then turn right down St Mary's Lane towards the church. Turn left on reaching the road junction with the Fire Station on the right and walk uphill back to the Plough.

There is a telephone number on the church door if you wish to obtain a key.

Here, as elsewhere, there are reminders of the local airfield. Near the centre of the village is a memorial stone to 460 Squadron of the Royal Australian Air Force. They operated as a heavy bomber squadron from 1941 to 1945 and 900 Australian airmen gave their lives. The squadron roll of honour may be seen in the church along with the standards of 5 Squadron and 11 Squadron. The Royal Air Force Memorial Window commemorates the link between the airfield and the village over the years. The airfield closed in 1988 and the quarters are now a housing estate. Outside the village school is part of the tail of a Lightning supersonic jet fighter. This marks the association that was established with RAF Binbrook and carries the marking of 5 Squadron on one side and 11 Squadron on the other.

Morton
The Ship Inn

MAP REF: OS EXPLORER 280 (GR 808915)	WALK 8	DISTANCE: 2 OR 2¾ MILES

DIRECTIONS TO START: FROM THE A159 SCUNTHORPE-GAINSBOROUGH ROAD TURN OFF TO MORTON 1¾ MILES NORTH OF GAINSBOROUGH, JUST AFTER GOING UNDER THE RAILWAY BRIDGE. **PARKING:** THERE IS NO CAR PARK BUT THERE IS DESIGNATED PARKING IN FRONT STREET DIRECTLY OPPOSITE ST PAUL'S CHURCH. ALTERNATIVE PARKING MAY BE FOUND IN THE VILLAGE HALL CAR PARK IN DOG AND DUCK LANE BUT THERE IS A ONE-WAY SYSTEM.

Morton is an attractive place still retaining its village identity despite neighbouring the outskirts of Gainsborough and this is a lovely walk by the River Trent. Morton lies in a prominent loop of the river and at one time was a small port, hence the name of the inn. It has a fine 19th century church which was largely the gift of Sir Hickman Beckett Bacon, lord of the manor and premier baronet of England. Thornock Hall, the home of the family after they moved from Gainsborough Old Hall, stood in a well wooded 300 acre park across the A159 where there was a large, well preserved Danish encampment, known today as Castle Hills. The tidal bore comes up the Trent here twice each day and more spectacularly during the spring tides. However, today it is sadly diminished since the great flood of 1947 scoured the river bed.

The Ship Inn

Entry to the pub is from the delightfully sounding Dog and Duck Lane. The ale on offer is John Smith's; there is also Carling Black Label and draught Guinness. It is a small roomed, beamed pub with traditional furnishing and an unfussy atmosphere. There is a games room with a pool table, a comfortable lounge bar and a small No Smoking dining area. The Ship is open from 12 noon to 11 pm Monday to Saturday, except on Wednesday when it opens from 4 pm to 11 pm, and from 12 noon to 10.30 pm on Sunday. Meals are served from 12 noon to 2 pm except Wednesday, and 6 pm to 8 pm. On Saturday evening, though, meals are only served for parties of eight or more when they can have the dining room to themselves. All meals are freshly cooked to order. Telephone: 01427 613298.

PLACES OF INTEREST NEARBY

Gainsborough Old Hall is well worth a visit. The 15th century Baronial Hall forms the best part of the present hall. Telephone: 01427 612669

The Walk

① Starting from the parking opposite St Paul's church walk down Front Street towards the river with the Crooked Billet on your right. Continue forward to turn right at the narrow alleyway by Morton Bight with Floss Mill Lane on the left. Keep on the river bank that remarkably quickly becomes a countryside path.

In 1013 the Danish King, Swein Forkbeard, sailed up the river with his son Canute and made a winter camp here at Gainsborough. Swein died the following year and Canute inherited his father's crown and is remembered for his attempt to hold back the tide. Some say that it was actually the River Trent's tidal bore – the Aegir – that he tried to restrain, in a demonstration to his nobles that even kings were not all-powerful.

② Upon reaching the hillocks on the right, turn right off the embankment to follow the short, field-edge path until you reach Field Lane, here an unsurfaced track. Turn right along the track passing a lonely bungalow on the left.

This walk may be extended by $3/4$ mile simply by staying longer on the river bank and then turning right on an obvious path down to Field Lane.

Walkerith

Ings Lane

To Laughton

Field Lane

River Trent

② ③ ④

To A159

START ①

MORTON

The Ship Inn

To Gainsborough

N

- ◄ - -
Route Walk

The River Trent at Morton

③ On arriving at the farm entrance on the right, with a footpath signpost and a kissing gate, continue along the lane past the allotments over on the right and on to the main road. Turn right back towards the village.

④ On meeting the road junction continue straight forward along Walkerith Road with the village hall on your right. The road changes to Dog and Duck Lane. Turn left up Chapel Lane and through the narrow alley at the end of the lane to turn right by the small green, to proceed along Pump Alley on the right with its Cycling Forbidden signpost. You come out of the alley on Front Street where your car may be parked.

Louth
The Woolpack

MAP REF: OS EXPLORER 283 (GR 337880)

WALK 9

DISTANCE: 2¼ MILES

DIRECTIONS TO START: AVOIDING THE TOWN CENTRE, FROM THE LOUTH BYPASS TURN OFF THE A16 AT THE GRIMSBY ROAD ROUNDABOUT TO FOLLOW DOWN NORTH HOLME ROAD, RIGHT ALONG NEWBRIDGE HILL, THEN RAMSGATE ROAD AND STRAIGHT ON AT THE ROAD JUNCTION INTO RIVERHEAD. THE WOOLPACK IS ON THE LEFT AND THE NAVIGATION WAREHOUSE ON THE RIGHT.
PARKING: IN THE PUB CAR PARK OR BY THE CANAL BEYOND NAVIGATION WAREHOUSE.

A remarkably contrasting town and waterside walk from this 'jewel of a town' beloved by John Betjeman. Louth is situated on the eastern edge of the Lincolnshire Wolds in an Area of Outstanding Natural Beauty. It lies in a green valley where the Eastern Wolds come down to the Marsh, here at its widest, and it takes its name from the River Lud.

The canal which you follow for this peaceful stroll was authorised by Parliament in 1763 and it took seven years to complete. It quickly became a busy waterway, carrying large quantities of coal, grain, oil, seeds, timber and all kinds of building material bringing much trade and prosperity to the town. The Navigation Warehouse at Riverhead, directly opposite the Woolpack, has been extensively refurbished and is an interesting museum.

The Woolpack

The Woolpack is an imposing building that dominates this section of Riverhead. It is popular with visitors and locals alike for imaginative food served in the roomy lounge bar that can become crowded, but there is a quiet, snug bar just across the corridor. A sample bar menu offers garlic mushrooms and salad, ham and cheddar ploughman's, gammon and pineapple, and ham, egg and chips but there is much more extensive fare on the constantly changing blackboard menu. It is a CAMRA inn that proudly displays a number of different category beer festival awards. Bateman's XXXB Classic Bitter, Dark Mild and XB Best Bitter are on offer plus Greene King Triumph Bitter. There is also Guinness and Scrumpy Jack cider on draught. Opening hours are Monday to Friday 11 am to 3 pm and 5 pm to 11 pm, Saturday 11 am to 4 pm and 5 pm to 11 pm. On Sunday they open from 12 noon to 4 pm and from 7 pm to 10.30 pm. Meals are served from noon to 2 pm and from 7 pm to 9.30 pm. Telephone: 01507 606568.

Ticklepenny Lock on the old Louth canal

footbridge above the lock. Railway transport killed the canal and the last vessel passed through the locks in 1924.

② Walk diagonally right uphill over the clear path to the lane and Keddington village. Do not enter the village on the left but continue forward along the lane and

The Walk

① From the Woolpack inn car park turn left with the Navigation Warehouse on your right. Climb up the embankment by the wooden marker post labelled 'Riverhead' to walk along the tree-lined tarmac path. Turn right over the bridge at the first lock after 350 yards and continue forward on the attractive path with the canal now on your left. After about 900 yards turn left across the narrow

PLACES OF INTEREST NEARBY

At **Hubbard's Hills**, a mile to the west of the town, the River Lud winds through a wooded gorge, a natural park of some 40 acres given to the town by a benefactor. Parking available.

Legbourne Railway Museum at The Old Station, Legbourne, Louth is open from Easter to the end of September, Tuesday to Sunday and Bank Holiday Mondays, 10.30 am to 5 pm. Telephone: 01507 603116.

parallel to the canal on your right.

③ Turn right on reaching the road junction to climb the two-step stile where there is a signpost to take you back across the field to Riverhead with the canal now on your right.

④ Do not cross over the first bridge on your return journey or follow the signposted footpath to the left. Continue forward with the canal still on the right and do not cross the next bridge. Walk forward through the old industrial development to Thames

Street and continue until you reach the main road. Turn right here for a few yards to Navigation Warehouse which is well worth a visit.

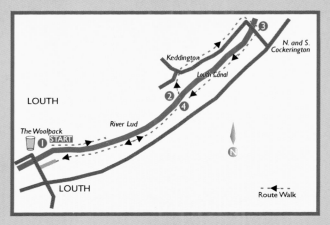

Scampton
The Dambusters Inn

MAP REF: OS EXPLORER 272 (GR 952793)	**WALK 10**	DISTANCE: $2^3/_4$ MILES

DIRECTIONS TO START: TURN OFF THE A15(T) LINCOLN TO SCUNTHORPE ROAD BY THE COUNTY SHOWGROUND ONTO TILLBRIDGE LANE (A1500) FOR $1^1/_2$ MILES AND THEN DOWN INTO SCAMPTON VILLAGE AT THE STAGGERED JUNCTION WITH THE VIEWPOINT ON YOUR LEFT. **PARKING:** IN THE PUB CAR PARK.

There are reminders in Scampton of the role it played in the Second World War, when the famous 617 Squadron trained here at the airfield for their mission to destroy the Ruhr dams in Germany and many other brave airmen played their part. But Scampton's history goes much further back. The road known as Middle Street, which takes you out into the countryside, is a prehistoric track, far older than the parallel Roman Ermine Street. An important Roman villa was also discovered in the area, near the Viewpoint, which seems later to have been used for a Saxon burial ground. Ancient and modern meet here, for today the Red Arrows are again based at Scampton and you may see them practising for their aerobatic displays and writing smoke trails in the sky.

The Dambusters Inn

There is a replica of the Barnes Wallis bouncing bomb used on the dams in the entrance and inside there are many photographs and exhibits relating to the wartime activities that took place from the nearby airfield. The inn is open Monday to Saturday 12 noon to 3 pm and 5 pm to 11 pm and on Sunday from 12 noon to 3 pm and 7 pm to 10.30 pm. Meals are served from 12 noon to 3 pm and 5 pm to 11 pm and on Sunday from 12 noon to 3 pm and 7 pm to 10.30 pm, but à la carte from 7 pm to 10.30 pm. A new restaurant room overlooking a small pond has an immense table that can seat 16 but there is a pleasant dining room with small rectangular tables adjoining the bar with an unusual high level open fire as a room divider. Beer served is Greene King IPA Best Bitter, Ruddles Smooth Best Bitter and Greene King Abbot Ale. Lagers include Stella Artois and Carling Black Label with Blackthorn cider. The bar menu ranges from an assorted list of baguettes, omelettes and salads to steak and ale pie, chicken curry and Cumberland sausage with gravy. You will discover that the toilets are marked 'Pilots' and 'WAAF'. Evening meals are much more elaborate and booking is advisable. Telephone: 01522 731333.

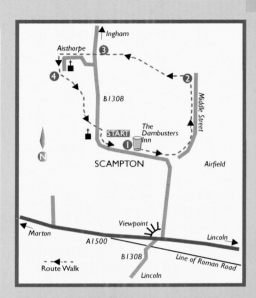

The Walk

① Turn left uphill out of the pub car park and at the bend in the road bear left to the end of tarmac. Continue forward for a few yards on the field edge until you turn left on the deteriorating tarmac of the very ancient Middle Street road alongside the airfield perimeter fence on your immediate right.

② Where a track comes in on the left leave Middle Street and walk downhill for 200 yards. There used to be a cottage here but it is difficult to establish the site today. Turn right off the track and go diagonally left across the field aiming for the right-hand end of the hedge where it bends northwards. On reaching the hedge turn left downhill to the bridleway bridge and signpost on the road.

③ Cross the road to follow the bridleway immediately opposite and carry straight

PLACES OF INTEREST NEARBY

Bransby Home of Rest for Horses is at Bransby village, just off the A1500 Tillbridge Lane (GR 900705). Free parking, picnic place and gift shop. Telephone: 01427 788464.

Scampton churchyard

on across the short arable field to the lane. Continue forward to turn left towards the church with the Old School House on the right. Walk past the church and bear left towards the bungalow.

④ Turn left over the concrete car space in front of the bungalow with the small stream on your left. Some 15 yards beyond the concrete hard standing turn right over a two-step stile and across the small paddock to another stile. Walk diagonally left towards Scampton church on a clear path. Upon reaching the hedge where another public footpath comes in from the left, continue forward aiming for the left-hand corner of the field, crossing the new drive to Scampton House en route. Turn right upon reaching the stile and lane with the cemetery and the graves of the German airmen on your immediate right. There are eight German graves from two planes shot down in the vicinity of the airfield. Walk round the bend in the road back to the Dambusters Inn.

Goulceby
The Threehorseshoes

MAP REF: OS EXPLORER 273 (GR 254791)	WALK 11	DISTANCE: 2¼ MILES

DIRECTIONS TO START: GOULCEBY IS 1½ MILES OFF THE A153 LOUTH TO HORNCASTLE ROAD AT SCAMBLESBY HILL, 7 MILES FROM LOUTH. DIRECTIONS TO THE PUB ARE SIGNPOSTED IN THE VILLAGE. **PARKING:** IN THE PUB CAR PARK.

Goulceby is a compact little village in an Area of Outstanding Natural Beauty, with a number of inter-linking public footpaths and an attractive ford. This pleasant stroll is along part of the Viking Way long distance path, field paths and country lanes. Red Hill may be seen as you walk downhill towards Manor Farm. This is a Lincolnshire Trust nature reserve open for visitors and is well worth a detour at the end of the walk. It is a fragment of chalk downland and an old quarry with many chalkland flowers such as yellow-wort, bee and pyramidal orchids and felwort. The reserve adjoins the road on the Raithby Road just above Manor Farm.

The Threehorseshoes

The Threehorseshoes was once a smithy. Forty years ago someone commented upon its 'homely charm and intimate atmosphere' and the intervening years have not altered that judgement. Mellow timbers, whitewashed walls and an ancient fireplace of hand-made Goulceby bricks all add to its atmosphere. From the external evidence it would seem that the house was built towards the end of the 18th century, though the extensive woodwork inside may indicate the refurbishing of a much earlier structure. Unfortunately the date stone, 1669, is nothing more than a practical joke by the late Ben Gray. Although it was not built as an inn, it is likely that the blacksmith found brewing a profitable side-line. Excellent bar snacks and restaurant meals are served. It is a real ale, free house serving Marstons Pedigree and Bitter plus a changing guest beer. Draught cider is available. It has a beer garden, a games room and a children's play area in the garden plus a small caravan and camping site. The opening hours are Monday to Saturday 12 noon to 3 pm and 7 pm to midnight, Sunday 12 noon to 3 pm and 7 pm to 11 pm. From Monday through to Sunday, except Tuesday, meals are available from 12 noon to 2.30 pm. However, sandwiches only are available on Tuesdays. Telephone: 01507 343610.

The Walk

① Turn right out of the pub car park down to the road junction and left for 120

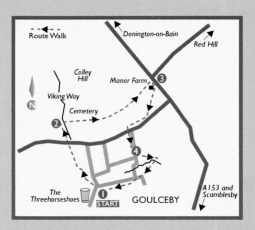

yards to a signpost and stile on the left. Walk diagonally left across the paddock to the field corner where there is a footbridge. Cross the bridge and follow the narrow footpath to the lane. Go over the lane and continue forward on the good track uphill until you reach the cemetery. This section is part of the Viking Way long distance recreational path.

② Just before reaching the cemetery gates leave the Viking Way to turn right on a signposted footpath that initially goes through the edge of the cemetery and then arable fields with a hedge on the right at first. Cross into the next field and aim downhill to Manor Farm to pass to the right of the farmhouse. There is a hedge on your left for this field.

PLACES OF INTEREST NEARBY

Rowgate Hill, Scamblesby, is a Countryside Agency Access Site. There are magnificent views over the valley of the River Bain from the top of Rowgate Hill, with a series of lynchets (ancient farming terraces) running along the side of the hill (GR 295787).

A quiet lane in Goulceby

③ Turn right on the lane for 50 yards, then right on the signposted footpath to walk diagonally left across the field, aiming to the left-hand field corner and just left of the prominent house. Turn right on reaching the lane and left at the T-junction to walk towards the village and downhill.

④ By the Shop Lane T-junction turn left on the signposted footpath with a newly created lake on the right. A few yards before reaching the track leading up to the house, turn right over the footbridge and then over a stile to walk straight forward to the lane. Walk down the lane and continue forward through the village until you reach the turn for the Threehorseshoes once again.

Alford
The Anchor Inn

MAP REF: OS EXPLORER 274 (GR 456762)	**WALK 12**	DISTANCE: $3\frac{1}{4}$ MILES

DIRECTIONS TO START: FROM THE A16 LOUTH TO LINCOLN ROAD TURN OFF FOR ALFORD AT ULCEBY CROSS. THE PUB IS SITUATED IN EAST STREET JUST BEYOND THE CHURCH. **PARKING:** THE PUB IS DIRECTLY OPPOSITE THE SHOPPING CENTRE WITH GOOD ALTERNATIVE PARKING, FOR THE CAR PARK AT THE INN IS SCHEDULED TO BE REDUCED IN CAPACITY DUE TO DEVELOPMENT.

Alford, dominated by its windmill, is a pleasant little town on the fringes of the Wolds with a long main street containing a number of hostelries, as befits a market town. The old thatched manor house, seen during the walk, unusually is almost in the town centre. The impressive church is chiefly 14th century, partly rebuilt in 1869. This small town, like many other places throughout England, was hit by the Black Death and some 132 townsfolk died including one unfortunate family who lost six members in a week. At nearby Tothby Manor a stone was placed with a hollow containing vinegar, where foodstuffs were exchanged and money left. The walk takes you past the windmill and out along country paths to nearby Thoresthorpe and Bilsby, returning through open fields.

The Anchor Inn

Known locally as 'The Pub with the Flowers' from its attractive window boxes, this is a real ale pub selling Batemans and Bass, Scrumpy Jack cider and draught Guinness. There is a No Smoking area, a beer garden and games room. Ramblers and cyclists are most welcome. There is a pleasant open dining room and their home-made steak and kidney pie is the most ordered meal. There is a daily specials board and the menu lists rib eye steak, Peking lemon chicken, ham, mushroom tagliatelle, and butterfly chicken with honey and mustard. Diane or pepper sauce is offered with all steaks. Sweets range from spotted dick, sherry trifle or bread and butter pudding to Italian tiramisu. Opening hours are Monday to Friday 11 am to 2.30 pm and 6 pm to 11 pm, Saturday 11 am to 2.30 pm and 6 pm to 11 pm and on Sunday 12 noon to 3 pm and 7 pm to 10.30 pm. Food is served from noon to 2.30 pm every day and in the evening from 7 pm to 9.30 pm on Monday to Saturday, and only until 9 pm on Sunday. Telephone: 01507 462062.

The Walk

① Turn right out of the pub car park and walk up the church path into the Main Street to turn right up Park Lane (not Park Road) with the thatched manor house on your left and a long, old wall. Park Lane is a cul-de-sac with a kissing gate leading to two footpaths at the end. Turn right after the kissing gate on through the thicket and then along the

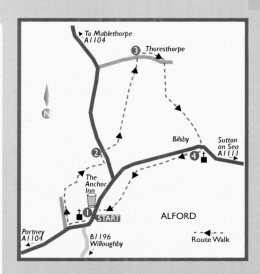

field edge to the road with the hedge and windmill on your right.

② Turn left on the roadside path for 75 yards and then cross the road to the stile and signpost to follow the field-edge path down to the footbridge, with a handrail in the right-hand field corner. After crossing the bridge walk straight forward uphill to an ancient tree and a three-way metal signpost. From here head diagonally right aiming for the gable of the right-hand farmhouse on the lane below.

PLACES OF INTEREST NEARBY

Alford Windmill has five sails and four pairs of stones, working on open days, wind permitting. Cream teas served. Open Saturday all year except Christmas and New Year, 11 am to 5 pm; July to August, Tuesday, Friday and Sunday, 1 pm to 5 pm.

Claythorpe Water Mill and Wildfowl Gardens at Aby with Greenfield is a beautiful 18th century water mill. Tea room and gift shop. Open beginning of March to end of October, 10 am to 6 pm. Telephone: 01507 450687.

Alford Mill seen from the walk

④ Cross the road where the footway narrows to follow the signposted path with kissing gate and churchyard on the left. Follow this attractive path down to the concrete bridge with handrails over the beck, cross the drive where there is a stile and signposts and then, walking parallel with the road, a whole series of stiles within sight of one another. On reaching the track crossing your front climb the stile and continue in the next field nearer to the road at the field edge. On reaching the house turn left for a few yards to find yet another stile in the corner with the garden on the right.

③ On reaching the lane turn right with the Cottage Nurseries on your left. Turn right off the lane on the signposted public footpath opposite the end of the high wall. Walk uphill to the telegraph post and then continue forward to the next post, ignoring the telegraph line on the right. At the hillcrest follow the line of posts to the far left corner of the field. Upon crossing into the next field do not follow the field-path edge but walk diagonally left across the field aiming for the middle of the three bungalows where you will discover a narrow, boarded path between the gardens. At the main road turn left down to the bridge over the beck.

Go diagonally right across the pasture field to a gap and stile about half way down the hedge. Cross the stile and turn left to the bottom of the grass paddock where there is a stile and signpost. In this next field turn diagonally right to the field corner aiming for the house with the pointed roof. There is a stile in the field corner, with footbridge and waymark. Turn right for 5 yards and then left up the tarmac path. Walk along Mill Close development towards the church. Turn right down Millers Way to the Anchor Inn.

Fiskerton
The Carpenters Arms

DIRECTIONS TO START: FISKERTON LIES SOME 5 MILES EAST OF LINCOLN, ON A MINOR UNCLASSIFIED ROAD. **PARKING:** IN THE PUB CAR PARK. THE OLD PRIMARY SCHOOL ON FERRY ROAD IS NOW USED AS A VILLAGE HALL; ALTERNATIVE PARKING ON THE FORMER PLAYGROUND HAS BEEN NEGOTIATED.

Fiskerton is situated on the northern bank of the River Witham. Nowadays the sole crossing of the river in the 12 mile stretch to Bardney is here at Five Mile Bridge, but this is only a high level pedestrian bridge. A riverside stroll at the beginning, there are no steep inclines during the walk except for the River Witham embankment. Then largely along peaceful green lanes or public footpaths over arable fields, the route passes the remains of the now abandoned Second World War airfield. It can be muddy in some sections after rain.

Three fisheries were mentioned at Fiskerton in the Domesday Book, a clear indication of how it got its name. Archaeologists have unearthed substantial remains dating back to the Stone Age, and one of the finest pieces of Anglo-Saxon jewellery in the country was found when the river was deepened in 1826. The brooch is now in the British Museum.

The Carpenters Arms

The Carpenters Arms has a pleasant snug bar favoured by locals and a lounge bar next to the attractive dining room extension. It is a real ale, free house serving Ruddles Ales and John Smith's, plus guest beers. Lagers are Fosters, Kronenbourg and Millers. Draught Guinness and Strongbow cider are also on offer. There are outdoor picnic tables on a patio by the restaurant at the rear of the pub. It offers an extensive range of starters, main dishes including fish, curry and vegetarian dishes, and home-made pies. One pie is known as Desperate Dan's and there is a selection of sweets. There is also an imaginative bar menu including one for children. The pub is not open at lunchtime Monday to Thursday. Its opening hours are Monday 7 pm to 11 pm, Tuesday to Thursday 5 pm to 11 pm, Friday 12 noon to 3 pm and 5 pm to 11 pm, Saturday 12 noon to 11 pm, Sunday 12 noon to 10.30 pm. Meals are served Tuesday to Thursday 5 pm to 9.30 pm, Friday 12 noon to 2.30 pm and 5 pm to 9.30 pm, Saturday and Sunday 12 noon to 3 pm and 7 pm to 9.30 pm. Telephone: 01522 751806.

The Walk

① From the Carpenters Arms turn left along the road with the village post office on your left. Turn left up Nelson Road by the post office corner for 50 yards and then right over the stile on the signposted narrow hedge-lined path. On reaching the field go over the ditchboard and turn right down towards the river. Cross the bridge

PLACES OF INTEREST NEARBY

Chambers Wood Nature Reserve has waymarked forest walks. Leaflets available, free parking and toilets (GR 141746, via Short Ferry).

over the drain and climb the river embankment to turn left with the River Witham on your right. Go over the stile at the end of the path with Five Mile Bridge on your right. Turn left down the good track to the road.

② Turn right on Ferry Road for 500 yards and then cross the road to a stile and signposted footpath. After climbing the second stile walk straight forward across the field, aiming for the right-hand edge of the wood. Continue straight on with the wood on your immediate left.

Turn right at Hall Lane for the longer walk and continue for 600 yards to turn left down a signposted concrete track. Do not take another bridleway to the right after 350 yards but continue forward with the hedge on your immediate left until you reach the green lane.

Upon reaching Hall Lane for the *shorter walk* you must turn left and continue to Hall Farm. Turn right off the lane by the farmhouse onto the signposted public footpath and across the waste ground to a stile. Follow the clear path with the hedge on your immediate right until you reach the green lane. Turn left here onto the route of the longer walk.

③ Turn left on the green lane and continue left at the track junction for just over 3/4 mile, passing the footpath for the shorter walk on your left en route.

The wartime airfield has been abandoned although some of the

Five Mile Bridge at Fiskerton

remaining concrete runways may still be seen, and the Cold War underground installations of 15 Group Royal Observer Corps and the United Kingdom Warning and Monitoring Organisation have only recently been closed down.

④ On reaching Hall Lane walk straight on to turn right on the signposted path on the right and across the pasture field to another stile. Turn diagonally left on a clear path to a stile by the housing development. Climb the stile and follow the very narrow path with the garden on your left. On reaching the end of the cul-de-sac turn left to the road and then right along the road back to the pub round the bend on the left.

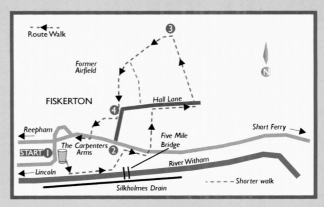

Halton Holegate
The Bell Inn

MAP REF: OS EXPLORER 274 (GR 417653)

WALK 14

DISTANCE: $2^3/_4$ MILES

DIRECTIONS TO START: HALTON HOLEGATE IS 3 MILES EAST OF SPILSBY ON THE B1195 WAINFLEET ROAD. **PARKING:** THERE IS VERY LITTLE SPACE FOR PARKING IN THE VILLAGE BUT IT IS POSSIBLE TO LEAVE YOUR CAR AT THE BELL WITH A COURTESY NOTE.

Halton Holegate is a charming village with an unexpectedly large Marsh church built of greenstone with a lovely proud pinnacled tower. The village overlooks the Marsh on the southern edge of the Wolds between the small market town of Spilsby and the River Lymn. It is said that this is the river of Alfred, Lord Tennyson's *Song from the Brook* with its familiar opening verse:

I come from haunts of coot and hern
I make a sudden sally
And sparkle out among the fern
To bicker down a valley.

The village looks across the Fens to Boston Stump some 15 miles away. The place name is descriptive for it refers to the hollowgate, being the road as it drops down to the valley. This deep cutting is visited during the walk, which heads out to Halton Bridge and towards Ashby by Partney before returning along the river.

The Bell Inn

This picturesque, prettily placed pub at the head of the cutting is a gem of a village inn, low beamed, friendly and well run by very experienced licensees. John was an Army chef for many years and enjoys making pies but most of all he takes great delight in serving a delicious fish soup. Memorabilia of two wartime Lancaster squadrons of the RAF, 44 and 204 formerly based at the nearby Steeping Airfield, decorate the walls of the pub. The Bell is a free house selling our local Bateman's Beer, Blackthorn cider and draught Guinness. Tables outside the pub offer opportunities for outdoor drinking when the weather is kind. Well behaved dogs are permitted. Meals are served from 12 noon to 2.30 pm and 7 pm to 10 pm Monday to Saturday, and to finish an hour earlier on Sunday. Drinks are on offer from 12 noon to 4 pm and 7 pm to 11 pm Monday to Friday, except Wednesday when it is noon until 3 pm and then 7 pm to 11 pm. Saturday hours are 12 noon to 5 pm and 7 pm to 11 pm, Sunday 12 noon to 4 pm and 7 pm to 10.30 pm. Telephone: 01790 753242.

The Walk

① From the Bell Inn car park turn right along the road back towards Spilsby and have a look at the information board on the right. Cross the road into Station Lane and after only a few yards turn left onto a signposted footpath. Go over the stile and walk straight forward towards the church with the school elm tree on your left. Take

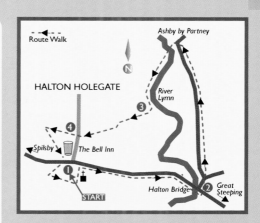

the footpath stile on your left and proceed into the churchyard. Walk through the churchyard and back down to Firsby Road. At the road turn right and walk with extreme care through the hollow way to cross the road as soon as possible to gain the walkway on the other side. Continue along this walkway for 1,200 yards.

② Turn left at Halton Bridge and then left again along the pleasant country lane leading to Ashby by Partney. After 1,400 yards when the lane turns sharply right turn left on a clear, signposted path down to a stile. Cross the paddock to another stile and concrete bridge and then bear left over the field to follow the river.

PLACES OF INTEREST NEARBY

At **Old Bolingbroke** the castle was destroyed after the Civil War and only a fragment remains but it is still a pleasant village to visit and there are some special roses on the village triangle.

The **Lincolnshire Aviation Heritage Centre** at East Kirkby, near Spilsby, has a large visitor centre and all-weather attractions. Situated on the A155. Telephone: 01790 763207.

The River Lymn

③ After 900 yards where the river turns distinctly to the left, turn right off the river bank to a stile with a waymark. With your back to the stile as the starting point walk diagonally right uphill until you sight a waymark on the right and then a footbridge and stile. Cross the bridge and in the next field still walking uphill aim slightly left towards a group of four poplar trees and later an electricity post with a waymark. From here walk forward to the left-hand corner of the field with a large residential home on the left until you reach Northorpe Road.

④ On reaching the lane turn right for a few yards and then go down a delightful track labelled Highfield Lane. Go through the metal gate to turn left on the signposted path downhill to the left-hand corner of the field by the farm buildings, where you will discover a stile. Cross the stile and with the farm buildings on your immediate right walk over the paddock to another stile and you will arrive back at the Bell Inn.

Skegness
The Vine Hotel

MAP REF: OS EXPLORER 274
(GR 565623)

WALK 15

DISTANCE: 1³/₄ MILES

DIRECTIONS TO START: FROM THE JUBILEE TOWER IN SKEGNESS TURN RIGHT ALONG DRUMMOND ROAD FOR 1 MILE. THE VINE HOTEL IS PROMINENTLY SIGNED ON THE RIGHT ON VINE ROAD CUL-DE-SAC.
PARKING: ON EITHER SIDE OF THE CUL-DE-SAC AT THE END OF VINE ROAD.

This walk is a totally unexpected countryside stroll down the Donkey Path that beach donkeys used when homeward bound each evening. The 9th Earl of Scarborough, the chief landowner and Lord of the Manor, had the foresight to see the possibility of developing Skegness as a seaside resort. In 1881 he built and opened the fourth longest pier in the country and anticipated modern town planning with a number of pleasant tree-lined avenues. In 1908 an artist, John Hassall, sold to the Great Northern Railway Company the painting which has become famous ever since as a poster, depicting a joyous fisherman bounding over Skegness sands with the caption 'Skegness is so Bracing'. The artist had never been near Skegness but that one picture did more to popularise the place than could ever have been imagined.

The Vine Hotel

The Vine is a long established hotel that has catered for visitors for well over 200 years. In 1813 it advertised 'Two good bathing caravans and a warm bath at any hour of the day. A neat post-chaise, good horses and a careful driver.' Alfred Tennyson, the future Poet-Laureate came as a youth to enjoy the solitude of the sand dunes and the cries of the wild fowl between Seacroft and Gibraltar Point. One farmer who knew him then said, 'I' them daays we thowt he wur daft. He was allus ramblin' off quite by hissen, wi'out a hat i' his hand or owt.' Today there is a bust of the poet in the Tennyson Lounge. The hotel brochure states: 'Tennyson used to sit in the gardens just waiting for Bateman's Good Honest Ales to be invented.' The lounge bar has an open fire, oak tables, and traditional real-ale hand pulls. There is an Oak Room with barrel stools and a collection of Bateman memorabilia. The lunchtime menu lists 79 items, including roast turkey and cranberry sandwiches and hot or cold cobblers. The hotel is open for meals all week from 12 noon to 2 pm and 7 pm to 9 pm. Drinks are available Monday to Saturday from 11 am to 3 pm and 7 pm to 10.30 pm. Sunday hours are 12 noon to 3 pm and 7 pm to 10.30 pm. Telephone: 01754 763018.

The Walk

① Turn right if you are coming out of the Vine to follow the attractive, tree-lined meandering track for some 450 yards.

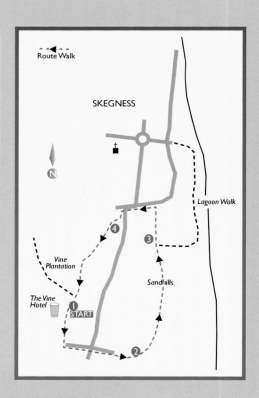

Turn left on reaching Seacroft Drive although the footpath is signed to continue across the road. Walk down to the main road and cross to continue straight forward up Drake Road with the golf links and club house on your right.

PLACES OF INTEREST NEARBY

Gibraltar Point National Nature Reserve is just down the road beyond Vine Road. The reserve is open all the year round from dawn to dusk. There is a visitor centre, with restricted opening during winter months. Telephone: 01754 762677.

Natureland Seal Sanctuary on North Parade, Skegness is open daily, November to March 10 am to 4 pm. Telephone: 01754 764345.

The path leading to the sandhills

Continue forward at Seacroft Esplanade on the footpath through the sandhills.

② Turn left at the good track at the edge of the sandhills or, if you so wish, further down the beach by the sea shore and continue for 800 yards.

③ By the car park at the end of Lagoon Walk turn left with the prominently labelled toilet block on your immediate left. Cross South Parade and continue straight forward down Barbara Road to turn left along Drummond Road.

④ After 80 yards cross the road to follow the signposted, winding tree-lined Donkey Path for ¼ mile. The path is quite another world from the image of holidaymakers on crowded seaside beaches. The Vine Hotel is round a final bend in the path.

Revesby
The Red Lion

MAP REF: OS EXPLORER 273 (GR 300615)	**WALK 16**	DISTANCE: 2¾ MILES

DIRECTIONS TO START: REVESBY VILLAGE IS ON THE A155 CONINGSBY TO SPILSBY ROAD, SOME 6 MILES FROM CONINGSBY. **PARKING:** IN THE PUB CAR PARK.

Revesby is a compact tree-shaded village, planned horseshoe wise, with a spacious sycamore-edged village green surrounded by almshouses built in 1862, but on the site of earlier almshouses erected in 1728. In the church is a quite magnificent 18th century memorial to the Banks family, including Sir Joseph Banks. He is remembered with the engineer Rennie for the drainage of the Fens and he sailed with Cook in the *Endeavour* in 1768 and assisted in the exploration of Australia. There is a splendid park at Revesby and a great house known as Revesby Abbey, not to be confused with the Cistercian abbey that stood ½ mile south of the church. Sadly Revesby Abbey is now derelict and nothing remains of the Cistercian abbey, dissolved in 1539, 400 years after its dedication. The site is passed on the walk to the Catchwater Drain, before returning along a country road.

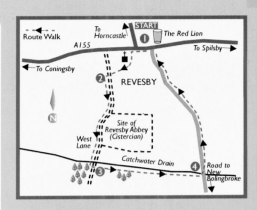

The Red Lion

The Red Lion is a Bateman's house. It
has a spacious bar with an open fire in
season and a pleasantly decorated
non-smoking restaurant. The normal
range of Bateman's ales are on offer
plus a guest beer, Scrumpy Jack cider
and draught Murphy's Stout. Chilled
wine is also available. There is a
games room, a beer garden and
children's play area. Closed on
Monday, the pub is open from
Tuesday to Friday from 12 noon to
3 pm and 6.30 pm to 11 pm. On
Saturday it is open from 11 am to
3 pm and 6.30 pm to 11 pm, Sunday
12 noon to 3 pm and 7 pm to
10.30 pm. Meals are served from
12 noon to 2 pm from Tuesday to
Sunday and 7 pm to 9 pm, with a
two-course, reduced price meal for
senior citizens on Fridays. There is a
children's menu and vegetarian
dishes, with fresh Grimsby fish on
Wednesday and Thursday and a
traditional lunch each Sunday. Dogs
are not permitted. Telephone: 01507
568665.

② Follow this track known as West Lane
until you reach the large bridge over the
Catchwater Drain. Good map readers with
a local Ordnance Survey map will realise
the correct route of the definitive public
right of way is on the north side of this
drain. However, a diversion application is
to be processed and the landowner has
accepted that the good track along the
southern bank will become the right of
way.

③ Therefore cross the West Lane bridge
and turn left with the Catchwater Drain
now on your immediate left and continue
until you reach the road and another
bridge.

The Walk

① Turn right out of the Red Lion car park
along the footway for 450 yards and then
cross to the lane leading up to St
Lawrence's church with the village green
on the left. At the end of the almshouses
on your right turn right through a kissing
gate onto a signposted path. Cross the
paddock diagonally left to a two-step stile
and a new footbridge over the ditch and
turn left down the good track.

PLACES OF INTEREST NEARBY
The Stickford **Allied Forces Military Museum**, on
the main road, is open Monday to Friday 9 am to
4 pm. Telephone: 01205 480317.

Tattershall Castle opens 30th March to the end
of October 10.30 am to 5 pm, 4 pm closing
November and December. Telephone: 01526
342543.

The village green at Revesby

④ Turn left along the road walking towards the traffic and either continue straight forward until you reach the A155 and the Red Lion, or turn left into the village green and the church to then retrace your steps of the earlier route.

Stickney
The Rising Sun

<table>
<tr><td>MAP REF: OS EXPLORER 261
(GR 344568)</td><td>WALK 17</td><td>DISTANCE: 3½ MILES</td></tr>
</table>

DIRECTIONS TO START: STICKNEY IS ON THE A16(T) GRIMSBY TO BOSTON ROAD, 8 MILES FROM SPILSBY. **PARKING:** IN THE PUB CAR PARK.

The Greenwich Meridian line is crossed twice during this lovely walk. This is the place to enjoy magnificent cloudscapes, beautiful sunsets and clear starlit nights. In summer it is a land of plenty but in winter when the flat fields seem to stretch for eternity you may get the feeling that the days when it was all marsh are not far away. Several attempts were made to drain the marshes and nearby fenland but were unsuccessful until the 19th century. Sir Joseph Banks of Revesby was an important promoter of the project. The Medlam River was straightened and a new drain, known today as the West Fen Catchwater Drain, was made. Roads were built along the top of the banks of the waterways – long, straight roads exposed to all the winds that blew – and beautiful brick bridges high enough for packet boats to pass underneath on their way to Boston market.

The Rising Sun

The Rising Sun has been a pub since 1846 although the building is almost 300 years old. It is a popular village local with unspoilt simplicity and truly old fashioned standards of welcoming hospitality in this free house serving Bateman's XB Bitter and Dixon's Olde Honesty as a guest beer, Foster lager and draught cider. There are low beams, horse brasses and local photographs, with a family room, a games room with darts and pool and a beer garden. Well behaved dogs are permitted. Bar meals range from a chip butty to prawn and mayonnaise sandwiches. Restaurant meals list soup of the day, prawns on a bed of lettuce, melon with port or smoked mackerel as starters, various steaks, chicken breast and beef curry as main course dishes with vegetarian options. Apple pie is amongst the desserts.

The pub is open Monday to Saturday from 11 am to 11 pm and on Sunday from 12 noon to 10.30 pm. Meals are served from 12 noon to 2 pm and 7 pm to 9 pm except on Sunday and Monday evenings. Telephone: 01205 480965.

The Walk

① Turn right immediately from the pub car park to walk down the track towards the mill for 60 yards, and then turn right over a footbridge with a waymark post. Go diagonally left across the paddock to another footbridge. Go to the left of the house (waymark) with a hedge on your right. Cross the next field diagonally left.

PLACES OF INTEREST NEARBY

Snipedales Country Park lies north of the B1195 between Spilsby and Horncastle. There are 210 acres of waymarked trails leading through both the nature reserve and the country park where you can enjoy ponds, broad open rides and steep sided valleys. Open all the year. Admission free. Charge made for car parking.

In the third field go diagonally left to a two-step stile leading on to a good track. Turn right to the road.

② At the road turn left down to the road bridge over the East Fen Catchwater Drain. Turn left on the village side of the drain along the top of the embankment until you reach the splendid wooden footbridge. Turn left and then right over a stile. Cross the field to the stile in sight in the fence. Continue forward past a derelict building with a hedge on the right to a footbridge in the right-hand field corner. There is another stile by the abandoned house. Turn right after the stile and then left by the outbuildings. Upon reaching the abandoned railway footbed do not turn left immediately but continue forward for a few yards to follow the attractive meandering path to the left and through the picnic area. Near to the road there are toilets and car parking.

③ Cross the road and take the clearly signposted footpath with commercial building on the left. Follow the footpath round until you reach West Fen Lane. Where this footpath meets the lane is the exact place of the line of the meridian. Turn right for a few yards only and then left along a motorable track down to Musgraves Bridge.

West Fen Catchwater Drain

④ Cross the bridge over West Fen and turn left with Musgraves Farm on your right. On a clear day you will be able to see Revesby from the bridge. Continue forward with the drain on your immediate left, through the wooden fieldgate, until you reach the tarmac track leading to the farmhouse and on to Stickney Bridge. Turn left towards the village passing West Fen Lane on the left. By the village hall you cross the meridian line once again. On reaching the main road turn right back to the Rising Sun.

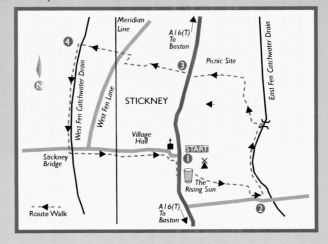

Digby
The Red Lion

DIRECTIONS TO START: DIGBY LIES TO THE EAST OF THE B1188, NORTH OF SLEAFORD. **PARKING:** IN THE PUB CAR PARK.

Digby is an attractive village with whitewashed cottages beyond the village hall, a wayside cross, a little round village lock-up like a pepperpot hardly big enough to stand up in, and a church going back to Saxon times. The walk starts well by crossing a clapper bridge over a rapidly flowing beck, and takes in the neighbouring villages of Dorrington and Bloxholm. There is also the opportunity to see one of the many sculptures in wood that North Kesteven District Council have arranged to be displayed at various points throughout the district.

The Red Lion

This is an interesting village pub that has managed to preserve a cosy and old fashioned traditional feeling with quiet little rooms but a surprisingly roomy restaurant. It is a Pubmaster house with ample parking, a No Smoking area, a games room, a family room, and there are ambitious plans to reconstruct the beer garden. Worthington and Adnam's real ale is served, plus draught Woodpecker and Scrumpy Jack cider. There is good value simple food such as lasagne, scampi or gammon steak, chips and peas (with egg or pineapple). Sweets include spotted dick and custard, ginger pudding and lemon sauce or apple pie and custard. It is advisable to book for Sunday lunch. Drinks are available from 12 noon to 2 pm throughout the whole week with an extra hour on Sunday. From Monday to Friday opening hours are from 7 pm to 11 pm, from 6 pm to 11 pm on Saturday and from 7 pm to 10.30 pm on Sunday. No food is served on Monday but from 12 noon to 2 pm throughout the rest of the week, including Sunday. Evening meals are from 7 pm to 9 pm from Tuesday to Friday plus an extra hour on Saturday until 10 pm. Telephone: 01526 320490.

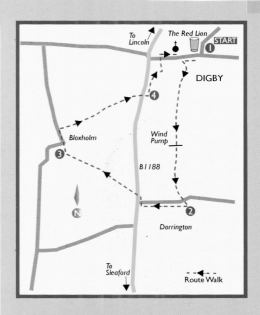

The Walk

① From the pub cross the road with the wayside cross to your right and follow the signposted path over the clapper bridge and then along Beck Farm wall with the beck on your right. Continue forward in a straight line keeping the small woodland coppice over on the left and aiming to the left of the prominent wind pump, where you will find a stile. Continue walking straight forward on the same line aiming eventually for the right-hand end of the line of houses and a narrow path by the garden to the entry road. Walk diagonally left across the playing field with the goal posts on your left to a signpost in the far left corner and a remarkable woodland sculpture.

PLACES OF INTEREST NEARBY

Dunston Pillar, to the north, was built in 1751 by Sir Francis Dashwood as a land lighthouse to guide travellers across the deserted heath. It was originally 92 feet high surmounted by a lantern. During the Second World War the Air Ministry decided that the pillar was a hazard to aircraft and possibly a landmark for German bombers and, as a result, it was reduced in height to 60 feet in 1941.

The village lock-up

② Turn right through Dorrington village for 700 yards until you reach the T-junction with the B1188 Lincoln road and the Musicians Arms on your left. Cross the main road to follow the signposted Road Used as a Public Path (RUPP) diagonally right across the field to Bloxholm. Upon meeting the farm track turn right along it into the village.

③ Walk straight forward down the village street, past Home Farm and the church on the left. After 300 yards turn right off the lane by the village hall to follow the good stoned track for ³/₄ mile to Gate House.

④ Turn left along the road verge for 350 yards into Springwell Hollow. Turn right off the road over a stile on the signposted path and diagonally left to the corner of the field by the council houses. Follow the tarmac path on the left to the village street. Turn right up the street with the church on your left and passing the village lock-up en route.

Fulbeck
The Hare & Hounds

MAP REF: OS EXPLORER 272 (GR 949505)

WALK 19

DISTANCE: $2^3/_4$ MILES

DIRECTIONS TO START: FULBECK IS BETWEEN GRANTHAM AND LINCOLN ON THE A607.
PARKING: PATRONS MAY LEAVE THEIR CARS IN THE LARGE CAR PARK AT THE HARE AND
HOUNDS BUT DO PLEASE LEAVE A NOTE INDICATING THAT YOU ARE DOING THE WALK
AND INTEND TO VISIT THE PUB ON YOUR RETURN. THERE IS ALTERNATIVE FREE PARKING
ON THE SPORTS FIELD CAR PARK OPPOSITE THE CHURCH LYCH GATE.

Fulbeck is long and narrow with the limestone heath east of the village and the heavier land in the Low Fields to the west. The Roman road, Ermine Street linking London, Lincoln and York, is the western parish boundary. Along the crest of the escarpment, and part of this walk, runs Pottergate, a far older prehistoric route that is part of the Jurassic Way, which follows the limestone belt across England from the Cotswolds to Yorkshire. The best of the village is off the main road behind the pub where a green opens to the church and there is a much restored village cross. The lanes throughout the village are steep and narrow, revealing dramatic views from many angles. The extensive view from the top of the escarpment along Pottergate is superb.

The Hare & Hounds

This country inn is a Grade II listed building built in the 17th century as a maltings and used as such until 1910. Accommodation is available in eight en-suite bedrooms overlooking the Courtyard Mews, including ground floor accommodation for disabled guests. There are two function rooms upstairs with original timbers exposed. The pine panelled lounge bar with roaring log fires in winter is a cosy place with an attractive view over the village green. Bar meals are traditional but include Lincolnshire specialities such as Poacher Cheese and Lincolnshire sausage. The pleasant dining room offers a full à la carte menu and a very extensive wine list. In the bar Woodpecker and Strongbow cider are on offer with a range of Bateman's ales and London Pride bitter. An unusual wheat beer Leaf Fall was very pleasant. There is a beer garden and the restaurant is a No Smoking area. Well behaved dogs are permitted in the bar. On Mondays to Fridays meals are served from 12 noon to 2 pm and 6 pm to 9 pm. Lunchtime meals are at the same time on Saturday and Sunday but evening meals are 7 pm to 10 pm on Saturday and 7 pm to 9 pm on Sunday. Telephone: 01400 272090.

The Walk

① From the Hare & Hounds car park turn left along the footway of the main road until you reach the new village sign just beyond the lych gate of the churchyard. Cross the road with care to the signposted public footpath along the left edge of the

PLACES OF INTEREST NEARBY

Manor Stables Craft Workshops are open daily from 10.30 am to 4.40 pm. Closed Mondays, except Bank Holidays.

Fulbeck Hall, rebuilt in 1733 after a disastrous fire, is the ancestral home of the Fane family, who have served England well as soldiers and administrators for many generations. It was the headquarters of the 1st Airborne Division in 1944 and there is an Arnhem Museum in the house commemorating the event of 'A bridge too far'.

sports field and continue to the left-hand corner of the field to a step stile. Cross the stile and walk uphill with the hedge now on your immediate right. Go over the abandoned railway line and continue straight forward uphill with the small reservoir nature reserve (no humans please) on your left. Continue uphill with the wood on your left and through the kissing gate to proceed along a pleasant hedged green lane to the ancient road called Pottergate.

② Turn right along Pottergate with Pottergate Farm, now a chairmaker's, opposite. Continue straight over the crossroads with the strangely named Gallipot Hall on your left and on the right the site of the Holy Well.

③ Turn right some 330 yards beyond the crossroads to follow the signposted public path, taking the path through the nursery not the parallel path leading to Holy Well Farm. Turn right at the end of the nursery path to walk past the farmhouse on your immediate left. Walk down the short bank and follow the hedge to a decrepit iron gate in the left-hand corner of the rough pasture. Continue forward downhill

The attractive village sign in Fulbeck

through a fieldgate and the remains of a hedge with the wooded line of the beck over on the right. In the last field aim for the right-hand end of the nursery buildings and then follow the broad track leading into the nursery until you reach South Heath Lane.

④ Turn left down South Heath Lane, crossing the line of the abandoned railway again, and towards the end of the lane follow the hard surfaced track on the right to cut off the corner

by the main road. Cross the road with care and the Hare & Hounds is on the right.

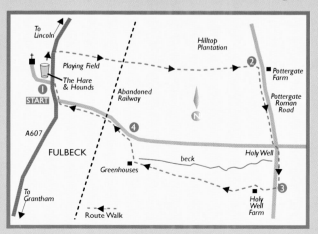

Cowbridge
The Cowbridge House Inn

<table>
<tr><td>MAP REF: OS EXPLORER 261
(GR 328471)</td><td>WALK 20</td><td>DISTANCE: 2¼ MILES</td></tr>
</table>

DIRECTIONS TO START: FROM THE BOSTON A16 ROUNDABOUT TAKE THE B1183 REVESBY ROAD WITH THE MAUD FOSTER DRAIN AND MILL ON THE RIGHT. COWBRIDGE IS 1³/₄ MILES ALONG THIS ROAD. **PARKING:** IN THE PUB CAR PARK.

This is a fascinating walk in an area that is a sort of aquatic Spaghetti Junction, where the main West Fen Drain converges upon Stonebridge Drain which carries the waters from the higher land. By an intriguing array of levels and sluices, the West Fen water can be allowed to pass under the catchwater and flow along the Cowbridge Drain to join that of the East Fen in Hobhole Drain. The whole is made more ingenious by the provision of a side cut in which there is a lock to allow the passage of boats from the West Fen to the Hobhole Drain.

The Cowbridge House Inn

The snug bar is equipped with football pennants and a large collection of baseball caps; yes, there is a Cowbridge Rangers Football Club. The pub has a garden area and well behaved dogs are permitted in the bar. The lounge has an attractive large dining area with waggon wheels being the focal point of the decor. The dining room is a No Smoking area. The menu is unusual and extensive. An example of a starter is green jalapeno peppers filled with cream cheese and coated in crispy crumbs. It is a real ale, free house offering meals from Tuesday through to Sunday from 12 noon to 2.30 pm and 7 pm to 10 pm, with no meals served at all on Monday. Opening hours are 11 am to 3 pm and 6 pm to 11 pm from Tuesday to Friday and all day on Saturday. On Monday the pub only opens in the evening, on Sunday from 12 noon to 3.30 pm and 7 pm to 10.30 pm. Drinks on offer were Home Mild, Home Bitter, John Smith's Extra Smooth, draught Guinness, Kronenbourg and Fosters lager and Scrumpy Jack cider. Telephone: 01205 362597.

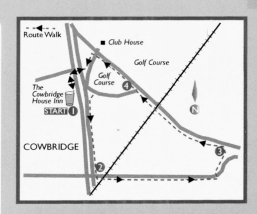

The Walk

① Cross the road in front of the pub and take the signposted path over the bridge across the Maud Foster Drain to turn right on the footpath and right again with the house on your right. Follow the clear bridleway at the side of the drain for 750 yards until you reach Rawsons Bridge.

② Turn left along the lane, over the railway crossing and continue for 1,100 yards. Take the first turn on the left up a cul-de-sac road just before your lane reaches the main road. Where your road bends sharply to the right walk straight on along a signposted footpath.

③ This path soon leads you alongside Cowbridge Drain on your right. Continue forward over the railway crossing and then a stile by a drain coming in from your left.

④ A footpath joins here from the left but

PLACES OF INTEREST NEARBY

The skyline of Boston is dominated by the tower of **St Botolph's church**, affectionately known as 'Boston Stump'. It is the largest parish church in England and was built in the 14th century. You are permitted to climb the 'Stump' and on a clear day are rewarded by a magnificent view over Lincolnshire and the Wash. Open every weekday, 9 am to 4 pm. The tower is closed on Sunday.

The **Maud Foster Windmill** was built in 1819 and is the tallest working windmill in England. It works daily when the wind blows producing stone-ground organic flour. It is open Wednesday 10 am to 5 pm, Sunday 2 pm to 5 pm plus Bank Holidays. Telephone: 01205 352118.

The aquatic 'Spaghetti Junction' at Cowbridge

continue to follow the Cowbridge Drain on your immediate right by descending the slope. The golf course is now on your left plus an embankment presumably to shield walkers from stray golf balls. Cross the bridge to your front (not the one on the right leading to the club house) and turn left immediately after crossing the bridge with Stone Bridge Drain now on your immediate left. At the end of the line of small trees and by a wooden electricity pole turn right across the fairway, aiming to the white concrete bridge and a white roadside fence. On reaching the road turn left back to the Cowbridge House Inn.

Sleaford
The Waggon & Horses

MAP REF: OS EXPLORER 271
(GR 075462)

WALK 21

DISTANCE: 1³/₄ MILES

DIRECTIONS TO START: TURN OFF THE A17(T) AT THE SLEAFORD MOOR SLIP ROAD JUNCTION WITH THE A153 SLEAFORD-HORNCASTLE ROAD (NOT AT THE HOLDINGHAM ROUNDABOUT) AND COGGLESFORD MILL IS ON THE LEFT ABOUT A MILE AFTER CROSSING THE RAILWAY BRIDGE.
PARKING: THE CAR PARK AT COGGLESFORD MILL. ALTERNATIVELY, THE DISTRICT COUNCIL OFFICES CAR PARK IS JUST ALONG THE ROAD AND IS AVAILABLE AT WEEKENDS AND OUT OF OFFICE HOURS.

Sleaford is believed to have been a medieval 'New Town' with the layout planned around the market place by local landlords. It was renowned for its stock of watermills. There were once up to a dozen in the town and more between Sleaford and Ruskington, but Cogglesford Mill is the only surviving watermill in Sleaford today and it is of enormous historical importance to the town. Until 100 years ago all the country's flour was produced by local wind and watermills but with the import of cheap grain from Canada and the United States of America little mills such as Cogglesford could not compete. The site of a watermill here is mentioned in the Domesday Book. The walk begins at the mill and follows the river into town, with refreshments at a pub near the Market Place. Market days are Monday, Friday and Saturday.

The Waggon & Horses

A well established town pub, literally a minute's walk from the Market Place. It has a large open bar, beams and a nicely timbered floor and clean looking bare rectangular tables that give the pub an unusual Scandinavian appearance and feeling of well being. On offer are Black Sheep Best Bitter, Bass, Worthington Cream Flow, draught Guinness and two lagers, Carling Black Label and Stella Artois. The nicely produced coloured menu is impressive, with such unusual starters as Giant New Zealand Mussels with a chilli and coriander crust, main courses such as fillet of salmon on a basil cream served with new potatoes and seasonal vegetables, plus sweets such as white chocolate, rum and raspberry trifle. There is also a blackboard menu offering special choices of the day and bar snacks. Meals are Monday to Saturday 12 noon to 2 pm and 7 pm to 9 pm except Thursday lunchtime. Saturday it is 12 noon to 3 pm and 7 pm to 9 pm. Sundays are 12 noon to 3 pm and 7 pm to 9 pm. It is wise to book for Sunday lunch. The pub opening hours are Monday to Saturday 11 am to 3 pm and 7 pm to 11 pm except Thursday when it opens 5 pm to 11 pm only. On Sunday the hours are 12 noon to 3 pm and 7 pm to 10.30 pm. Telephone: 01529 303388.

The Walk

① Starting from Cogglesford Mill car park turn left towards the mill, cross the bridge over the Slea and turn right to walk along

PLACES OF INTEREST NEARBY

North Ings Farm Museum is at Dorrington on the B1188, continue through the village centre for $\frac{1}{3}$ mile. It has a narrow gauge railway and steam/diesel trains. Admission charge. Telephone: 01526 833100.

the tow path. Continue as far as the bridge on your right.

② Keeping on the same side of the river continue forward along East Banks as far as you can with some attractive development on the right and more planned.

③ At the end of the Navigation you come to Carre Street. Cross the street and go under the arch at Mill Court to walk directly right across the large car park with the enormous Money's Mill (tourist office) on the left to an alleyway called Gladstones Yard Alley that takes you into Southgate, the main street. Turn right along Southgate for some yards and by the second stream passing under the road cross the road to turn left up Riverside with the stream on your immediate right, through some well designed new development and past a small bandstand on the left. Upon reaching the road turn right with the Rose and Crown across the road on your left. Turn left on reaching the main road again but only for a few yards until you reach the Lion Hotel. Cross the road here to go up an alleyway labelled Market Street. Turn left in the left-hand corner of the Market Square by a gate leading into the vicarage. After a couple of dozen yards turn right on reaching the lane with the offices of the Community

Cogglesford Mill

Council for Lincolnshire on your immediate right. Turn right through the attractive Vicars Court development which brings you out at the Waggon & Horses.

④ On leaving the pub turn left to walk along the road with the District Council offices across the road. At the end of the council car park on the right walk down the steps to follow the winding footpath back to the river and a bridge. Turn

left before the bridge back to the mill car park.

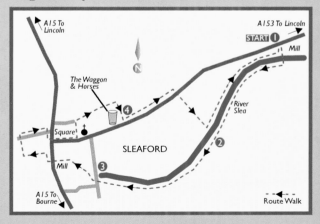

Helpringham
The Nag's Head

MAP REF: OS EXPLORER 248 (GR 140408)

WALK 22

DISTANCE: 2¼ MILES

DIRECTIONS TO START: TURN SOUTH OFF THE SLEAFORD-BOSTON A17 ROAD AT HECKINGTON AND FOLLOW SIGNS TO HELPRINGHAM FOR 3 MILES. **PARKING:** IN THE PUB CAR PARK. THERE IS POSSIBLE ALTERNATIVE ROADSIDE PARKING AROUND THE GREEN OR OUTSIDE THE VILLAGE HALL.

This is an easy stroll with wide horizons on the edge of the Fen. Helpringham with its red-tiled and slated roof cottages, spacious village green and medieval church has the classic look of an English village. On the western edge of the Fen between Sleaford and Spalding, the parish was crossed by the Roman Car Dyke canal and bounded on the east side by the South Forty Foot Drain. An interesting feature of the village is that it is surrounded by four bridges. It is an ancient place, for Iron Age saltings – evaporating pans for extracting salt – have been traced down North Drove. Dick Turpin the highwayman operated hereabouts and he was convicted at York of stealing a mare and foal from nearby Heckington. He was actually sentenced for another crime and executed at York in 1739.

The Nag's Head

The Nag's Head is a traditional village pub with quite a large bar and a seasonal roaring log fire, with a games annexe at the end of the bar including a pool table. There is a separate lounge and restaurant area with a No Smoking restriction in the dining room. At the rear of the pub is a large beer garden with picnic tables. Opening hours are 12 noon to 11 pm throughout the week including Sunday. The drinks on offer include Bass, Theakstone's XB, Adnam's Bitter, John Smith's Extra Smooth, Chestnut Dark Mild, draught Guinness, Fosters and Kronenbourg, Strongbow cider and nine wines. The pub is open for meals from Tuesday to Saturday from 12 noon to 2 pm and 6 pm to 9.30 pm. On Sunday meals are only served from 12 noon to 3 pm and it is wise to book. An imaginative, reasonably priced menu includes starters such as soup of the day, Buffalo Wings, garlic mushrooms and more. Main courses cover various steak dishes, Thai Tangy Chicken, fish dishes and salads with steak, chicken and bacon or prawn. Vegetarians are catered for with three different dishes. Basket meals are extraordinary good value. Telephone: 01529 421274.

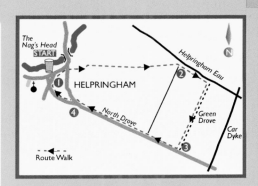

a Road Used as a Public Path (RUPP) which carries a higher status than a mere bridleway. This is a good track for most of the way but it peters out. Continue on the same line making for the left-hand junction of the hedge/dyke with the embankment of the Helpringham Eau.

② Climb the embankment and turn right with the river on your left. Continue for 350 yards until you arrive at Green Drove. Leave the embankment and turn right down the straight drove on a good track until you arrive at the lane known as North Drove after 750 yards. Fenland roads are so often dead straight and this one is a cul-de-sac ending at the River

PLACES OF INTEREST NEARBY

The Pea Room Craft Centre, Station Road, Heckington displays a collection of contemporary crafts including ceramics, textiles and jewellery. Open Monday to Saturday and Bank Holidays 10 am to 5 pm, Sunday 12 noon to 5 pm. Telephone: 01529 460765.

Heckington Windmill, also in Station Road, is a unique eight-sailed windmill now in working order. Admission charge. Open varying times. Telephone: 01529 461919.

The Walk

① Turn left on leaving the pub car park past the garage and cross the road to East Street. By the road junction take the signposted path on the left. It is signposted 'Bridleway' but officially it is

The village green at Helpringham

Farm Pumping Station on the South Forty Foot Drain.

③ Turn right along North Drove towards the village and the church with its prominent spire. Actually the map shows public rights of way in the fields on either side of the road but there is little traffic down the drove.

④ At the road junction walk straight forward along North Fen Road to the village green and then across the green to the Nag's Head.

Allington
The Welby Arms

| MAP REF: OS EXPLORER 247 (GR 858403) | **WALK 23** | DISTANCE: 4½ MILES |

DIRECTIONS TO START: ALLINGTON IS NORTH-WEST OF GRANTHAM, ACCESSIBLE FROM THE A1 OR A52. **PARKING:** IN THE PUB CAR PARK.

The Viking Way and an ancient lane make this enjoyable walk rather special. Allington is a quiet little village on the very edge of Lincolnshire. It possesses a small green outside the Welby Arms with the base and shaft of a 15th century cross. The village was owned by the Welby family for over 200 years hence the name of the pub. The church of Holy Trinity is almost concealed in the grounds of the Hall.

The Viking Way long distance recreational path goes through the parish but not the village, following here the very ancient Sewstern Lane, today an unsurfaced green lane. The lane is a prehistoric route running from the Welland valley and perhaps even from East Anglia to the river crossing at Newark and was used by hunter-gatherers long before the Romans came to our shores. There is always something rather special about walking in the footsteps of earlier generations lost in the mists of time.

The Welby Arms

The Welby Arms is a gem. It is an unspoilt pub with well kept beer and good value home-made food. There is a separate dining room with a No Smoking policy. It overlooks a pleasant, sheltered courtyard with hanging baskets. En suite accommodation is available centred around the courtyard. Drinks served are Draught Bass, John Smith's Bitter, Taylor Landlord and a long list of guest beers. There is also cider and draught Guinness. The bar has banquette seating with pleasant alcoves. It is a free house and dogs are not permitted. Meals are served from 12 noon to 2 pm and 6 pm to 9.30 pm every day. Booking on Sundays is essential. The pub is open from 12 noon to 2.30 pm and 6 pm to 11 pm from Monday to Saturday. On Sunday drinks are served from 12 noon to 3.30 pm and in the evening from 6 pm to 10.30 pm. Telephone: 01400 281361.

The Walk

① Turn left out of the pub car park along the Bottesford byway with the village green on your left and later the Manor House with its prominent Dutch gables. When the road turns sharp right by the village playing field proceed straight forward on the signposted public footpath and over to the left-hand corner of the field. Continue straight forward across the next field to a small footbridge and stile with an electricity pylon on the left. Cross the paddock to a stile with a waymark and then another waymark in the hedgeline to your front. Proceed across the large field, aiming initially for the gap between the two woods, with Glebe Farm over on the right. Aim later for the right-hand end of the right wood until you reach a stout wooden bridge with handrail and a footpath signpost.

② This is Sewstern Lane, on this section an unsurfaced track. Turn right along the green lane, cross the byway to Bottesford and walk down into the dip. As you are climbing out of the dip you will see a signpost and a hedgeline on the right.

③ Turn right off Sewstern Lane along this signposted public right of way with the hedge on your immediate right for 880 yards.

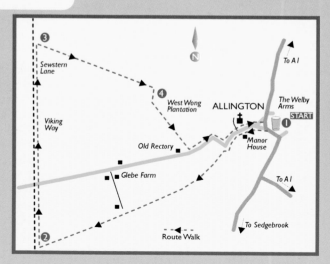

Ancient Sewstern Lane, now part of the Viking Way

④ Turn right over the stile onto another green lane, go round the bend and continue forward with West Wong Plantation on the left. Upon reaching the byway turn left to retrace your steps back into the village.

PLACES OF INTEREST NEARBY

Belton House, a National Trust property, is 3 miles north-east of Grantham on the A607. A magnificent house with formal gardens, an orangery, large park and adventure playground. Telephone: 01476 566116.

Belvoir Castle, 7 miles west of Grantham on the A607, is the seat of the Duke of Rutland. Open Easter to October (closed Monday and Friday). Telephone: 01476 870262.

Surfleet
The Mermaid Inn

| MAP REF: OS EXPLORER 249 (GR 251282) | **WALK 24** | DISTANCE: 2 MILES |

DIRECTIONS TO START: SURFLEET IS REACHED FROM A TURNING OFF THE A16(T) SPALDING-BOSTON ROAD, 2 MILES NORTH OF THE PINCHBECK ROUNDABOUT. **PARKING:** IN THE PUB CAR PARK.

Surfleet sits prettily on the banks of the little River Glen as it nears the end of its 31 mile journey to join the Welland. When the bulbs are in bloom this part of the fen is a sight to behold, making this easy riverside walk even more of a pleasure. The church of St Laurence stands at the crossroads just before the bridge and you are not seeing things, for the tower and spire really are out of true. Soon after its building in the 14th century the foundations of the church began to sink into the fenland soil with the result that the top of the spire is 6 foot $4\frac{1}{2}$ inches out of the perpendicular. Owing to the lean of the tower, two of the bells are technically outside the foundations of the church. Lying in the chancel is the 14th century figure of a knight in armour, his shield upon his arm. It is believed to be Sir Roger de Cressy of Cressy Hall, Gosberton.

The Mermaid Inn

This privately owned and managed inn has preserved the atmosphere of a traditional family hostelry catering for everyone from regular diners and locals to fishermen and walkers. In the spacious, separate dining area a range of home-made specials can be obtained, plus grills, fish dishes and a selection of desserts. Dogs are not permitted on the premises except guide dogs. Overnight accommodation is available. The inn is a free house serving real ale and beer was once brewed here. On offer is Fuller's Chiswick Bitter, John Smith's Bitter, Adnam's Broadside and Fenland Breweries Doctor's Orders. Stella Artois and Carlsberg lagers, draught Guinness and Stowford Press cider are also available. Stowell's of Chelsea Muscadet and Liebfraumilch wine can be served. There are no smoking restrictions in the inn. There is an extensive two-section car park and a pleasant garden overlooking the river with provision for out of doors drinking and a children's play area. From Monday to Saturday meals are served from 11.30 am to 2 pm and 6.30 pm to 9.30 pm, and on Sunday 12 noon to 2 pm and 7 pm to 9 pm. The inn is open Monday to Saturday 11.30 am to 2 pm and 6.30 pm to 11 pm, on Sunday 12 noon to 3.30 pm and 7 pm to 10.30 pm. Telephone: 01775 680275.

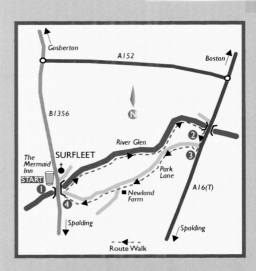

The Walk

① A 'can't get lost' walk! From the pub car park leaving by the main road entrance turn right to cross the bridge over the River Glen and immediately cross the road into Park Lane. On the left-hand side of the lane there is some waste ground with the possibility of alternative parking if required, a public footpath signpost and stile. This section of the route is part of three recreational walks – the Macmillan Way is a fully waymarked 290 mile coast to coast walk from Boston, Lincolnshire to Abbotsbury in Dorset and the other two, the Brown Fen Waterways Trail and the

PLACES OF INTEREST NEARBY

Pinchbeck Engine and Land Drainage Museum has a fine working beam engine of the kind used to drain the fens. Follow the brown signs off the A16, yellow signs off the bypass. Admission free. Open daily, April to October, 10 am to 4 pm.

Spalding Bulb Museum and Horticultural Exhibition is between Pinchbeck and Surfleet on the old A16. Free admission. Open April until October, 10 am to 4 pm.

The River Glen

Millennium Trail, are local walks initiated by South Holland District Council. Go over the stile and walk through the attractive grounds of the house, keeping as near as possible to the river bank. At the end of the garden go through the hedge and continue forward with the river still on your immediate left.

② After almost a mile, beyond the hedge you approach the busy A16(T) road with a pub prominent on the opposite river bank. Turn right on the signposted footpath for 200 yards.

③ At the vehicle-turning circle at the cul-de-sac end of Park Lane turn right down the narrow meandering track, passing Newland Farm on your left en route.

④ On reaching the T-junction with the main road cross the road and then the bridge, perhaps to walk on to the crossroads to look at St Laurence's church before returning to the Mermaid and a welcoming landlord.

Edenham
The Five Bells

MAP REF: OS EXPLORER 248, (GR 061219)	WALK 25	DISTANCE: 2¼ MILES

DIRECTIONS TO START: EDENHAM IS 3 MILES NORTH OF BOURNE ON THE A151.
PARKING: IN THE PUB CAR PARK. ALTERNATIVELY, AT THE VILLAGE HALL ON THE WALK ROUTE.

A hilltop walk with excellent views of the surrounding countryside and Grimsthorpe Castle. Edenham is situated in very pleasant rolling countryside, wooded by remnants of the old Kesteven Forest and watered by the Eden stream flowing southwards to join the River Glen. It is an attractive village with a few stone houses by the wayside and a magnificent church on its raised mound. There are some splendid cedars in the churchyard and a large, mainly Georgian vicarage where Charles Kingsley is said to have written *Hereward the Wake*. In the chancel of the church centuries-old grandiose monuments pay tribute to the noble family whose home is at Grimsthorpe Castle a mile away, Lincolnshire's finest country house. Part of the route is Countryside Agency funded access land and you are requested to please keep dogs on a lead where there is stock.

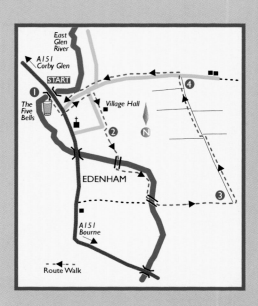

The Five Bells

The Five Bells is a square-built pub with mullioned windows said to have come from a demolished manor house. There is very friendly and accommodating service in the large attractive, carpeted lounge that boasts two open fires in season. The pub belongs to the Pubmaster group, serving Pedigree Tetley's real ales, draught Guinness and Blackthorn cider. Chilled wine is also on offer. It has a No Smoking area, a pleasant garden and a large well equipped playground for children. There is a wide range of food available from sandwiches to mini French sticks with cheese and pickle or baked jacket potatoes. Appetisers include button mushrooms cooked in lemon and garlic cream sauce on a bed of croutons. Grilled rainbow trout are among the range of fish dishes, or there is fruity chicken curry, home-made steak and kidney pie and vegetarian dishes such as spinach and ricotta cheese cannelloni, plus a large selection of sweet courses and coffee with mints. The pub is open Monday to Friday 11 am to 2.30 pm and 6.30 pm to 11 pm, Saturday 11 am to 3 pm and 6 pm to 11 pm, Sunday 11 am to 3 pm and 6 pm to 10 pm. Meals are available from 12 noon until 2 pm each day, and 7 pm to 9.30 pm from Monday to Friday, 6.30 pm to 10 pm on Saturday and Sunday. Telephone: 01778 591235.

The Walk

① Cross the main road to turn left up School Lane with the school on your left and then turn right up Church Lane. The village hall with possible alternative parking is on the left.

② Where Church Lane bends sharply to the right continue straight forward through the field gate and over the cattle grid on a good track. Cross the

PLACES OF INTEREST NEARBY

Grimsthorpe Castle is the centrepiece of a 3,000 acre park of rolling pastures, landscaped lakes and historic woodlands. The medieval deer park and Tudor oak park are crossed by fine avenues of trees – a haven for wildlife. There is an Oaks Nature Trail, a formal flower and topiary garden and a woodland adventure playground. Home-made teas are available in the Coach House. Open Sunday, Thursday and Bank Holidays from Easter Sunday until 24th September. Also daily in August. The park and gardens are open from 11 am to 6 pm and the castle from 1pm. Admission charge. Telephone: 01778 591205. Website at www.grimsthorpe.co.uk

East Glen River

concrete footbridge on the right over the East Glen River and turn left along the field edge with the river on your left. Recross the river at the next footbridge to walk uphill to the left-hand corner of Pillar Wood.

③ Turn left here across the field with the hedge on your immediate left for about 800 yards then left again over a stile just before reaching the field boundary to your front. Continue straight forward with the hedge now on your right over the unusual three-part stile and on to the lane.

④ On reaching School Lane, before walking steeply downhill pause to look at the splendid panorama from your height of over 200 feet with the castle in view about $1^1/_2$ miles away. Walk down the hill to the main road and your starting point but do seize the opportunity to look in the church.

South Witham
The Blue Cow Inn

MAP REF: OS EXPLORER 247 (GR 928191)	WALK 26	DISTANCE: 3½ MILES

DIRECTIONS TO START: SOUTH WITHAM IS WEST OF THE A1, 3 MILES SOUTH OF COLSTERWORTH. **PARKING:** IN THE PUB CAR PARK.

The village name comes from the River Witham which rises just across the Rutland border and here flows northwards on its 70 mile journey to the Wash, gathering many little streams from Rutland and Leicestershire on the way. To the west between the source of the river and the village is the spot where Lincolnshire, Rutland and Leicestershire meet. To the east is the Roman Ermine Street, later the Great North Road and today the A1 trunk road. The old village is predominantly of stone with some houses with moulded chimneys and mullioned windows but there are also a number of modern houses as the village has developed. Nearby Cottesmore is an operational RAF aerodrome and you may see and hear some spectacular aircraft taking off or landing during the walk for the first section actually takes you up to the landing guiding lights of the runway.

The Blue Cow Inn

Whoever saw a blue cow? Sir William Manners offered free ale on his properties to every tenant who promised to support the Whig candidate and the inn signs were painted blue as an extra election gimmick. There are a number of other 'blue' pubs in the neighbourhood which just goes to show far his writ must have run at that time. The Blue Cow is a traditional village inn with plenty of character serving beer from its own brewery at the rear of the premises. There is always a warm and friendly welcome in this civilised country pub a world away from the busy A1 just across the fields. It is open from 11 am to 11 pm from Monday to Saturday and 12 noon to 10.30 pm on Sunday. There is quite a large selection of wines available. Meals are served from 12 noon to 2.30 pm and 6 pm to 9.30 pm. Specialities include Cajun, Mexican, South American and Thai dishes as well as the whole range of home-made bar meals. The menu changes frequently with the seasons and it is displayed daily on a blackboard in the bar. Telephone: 01572 768432.

The Walk

① The public footpath actually goes from the rear of the car park. Take this path that leads you up the embankment to cross the old railway line. Go down the bank and ignore the path on the right that you will use later. Continue straight forward across the small field on a clear footpath and cross the county boundary

PLACES OF INTEREST NEARBY

Morkery Wood is a very large wood with public access, parking and a picnic site. It is a mile away across (under) the A1. (GR 956194).

Geeson Bros Motorcycle Museum and Workshop is at 2 and 4 Water Lane, South Witham, with 83 British bikes dating back to 1913. Refreshments in the workshop. Open 10.30 am to 5 pm on dates to be advised. Telephone: 01572 767280.

into Rutland. Walk over the Green Lane crossing your front and continue diagonally right across the large field aiming for the aircraft landing light cluster nearest the road as soon as they come into view, as you climb the gentle slope until you reach the New Road.

② Go straight across the road and then across the small field to a gap in the hedge – there is an overgrown bridge of stone in the shallow dyke. Walk forward across the field to the three-way footpath signpost. Turn right here to follow the clear route of the Viking Way to Thistleton village.

③ Turn right down the village street for 270 yards and on the outskirts of the village turn left. There is a stile immediately in front of you but at the moment of writing it is not the correct official route. Turn left down the track behind the houses to discover a kissing gate on the right after just over 100 yards. Go through the gate and keep to the edge of the grounds on the right until you reach the right-hand corner. This is the definitive public right of way at the moment. On entering the field proceed diagonally right to the quarry embankment where there is a stile and a

South Witham church

signpost. If you reach the embankment too early simply turn right along the fence until you meet the stile. There should not be any difficulty if the path has been reinstated. Walk inside the fence at the bottom of the embankment on a clear path that turns sharp left around the quarry boundary.

④ Turn right on meeting the line of the old railway and down to Thistleton Lane with the railway bridge on your left. Go straight across the road and continue up the path with the old railway still on your left. Climb up the

embankment and retrace your steps back to the Blue Cow Inn car park.

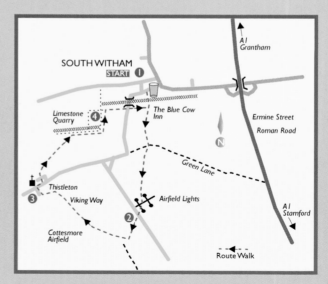

Tydd St Mary
The Five Bells

| MAP REF: OS EXPLORER 235 (GR 445187) | WALK 27 | DISTANCE: 2½ MILES |

DIRECTIONS TO START: TURN OFF THE A1101 LONG SUTTON TO WISBECH ROAD FOR ½ MILE TO TYDD ST MARY ABOUT 6 MILES NORTH OF WISBECH. **PARKING:** IN THE PUB CAR PARK.

An easy stroll in a fenland village along quiet lanes and a green lane labelled World's End. The Tydds, for there are more than one, are where three counties meet, Lincolnshire, Cambridgeshire and Norfolk. At the nearby Tydd Gote they have an awful joke with newcomers by explaining that Tydd Gote really means 'Tide Go Out'. Actually Tydd derives from teat, meaning that it stands on slightly higher ground. The tide up the River Nene, only a mile or so away, does however reach its limit in the area. Two great drains, the South Holland and the North Level, empty into the river hereabouts. The church is usually open and it is well worth a visit. It is said that Nicholas Breakspear (Adrian IV), the only Englishman ever to become Pope, was rector here in the 12th century. One of the stained glass windows in the church is to Robert Metcalf, who practised as a surgeon in the village for 53 years.

The Five Bells

This simple village pub has a new owner and their Sunday roast lunches are already deservedly popular. It is a real ale pub selling Abbotts Ales, Strongbow cider and draught Guinness. There is a new restaurant, a beer garden, a games annexe with a pool table and a juke box, a bar area with an open fire and a quiet room with television. There is a No Smoking area. Well behaved dogs are permitted. At the moment the Five Bells opening hours are 7 pm to 11 pm from Monday to Saturday and on Sunday 12 noon to 4 pm and 7 pm to 10.30 pm. However in June, July and August 2001 it is planned to open from 12.30 pm to 2.30 pm during the week. Telephone: 01945 420209.

The attractive village sign

The Walk

① From the pub car park turn left along the roadside footway walking towards the main road and then cross the road to take the track Mill Road leading up to Eastfield House with the graveyard on the right. Opposite the kissing gate and footpath signpost on the left turn right into the graveyard on the clear path. Walk through the graveyard and, if you have time, look into the interesting 14th century church. Go through the lych gate and down to Church Lane. Turn left along the road with the Five Bells over on the right. After 200 yards turn left at the Rectory Road junction.

② After ¼ mile where the road bends sharp right continue straight forward along World's End at first on tarmac and later, after the last

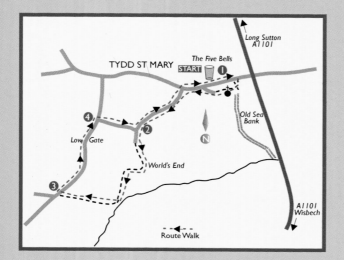

The church where Nicholas Breakspear, later Pope Adrian IV, was once rector

house on the left, on a grassy track. Walk on around various bends for almost ³/₄ mile until you reach the junction with Low Gate.

③ Turn right along Low Gate passing Low Gate House on the right, until you reach the other end of Rectory Road.

④ Turn right up the pleasant Rectory Road and follow the road round to retrace your steps to the Five Bells.

PLACES OF INTEREST NEARBY

At Terrington St Clements off the A17, west of Kings Lynn, the **African Violet Centre** is open daily with 4,000 blooms and a wide variety of types and colours. Telephone: 01553 828374.

The Butterfly and Falconry Park at Long Sutton is open daily. It is one of Britain's largest indoor butterfly gardens, with hundreds of exotic species flying free. The falconry centre houses owls, hawks and falcons. Check for the times of flying displays. Telephone: 01406 363833.

Baston
The Baskervilles

MAP REF: OS EXPLORER 235
(GR 118142)

WALK 28

DISTANCE: 3³/₄ MILES

DIRECTIONS TO START: TURN FOR BASTON OFF THE A15 BOURNE TO PETERBOROUGH ROAD 2 MILES NORTH OF THE MARKET DEEPING A16(T) ROUNDABOUT. **PARKING:** IN THE PUB CAR PARK. THERE IS THE POSSIBILITY OF ALTERNATIVE PARKING IN THE ROAD BY THE CHURCH.

Baston is an ancient place, an attractive Fen frontier village with a mixture of stone and brick houses, strung out for half a mile along the modern road leading to the extensive gravel workings. Its situation near King Street Roman Road and the Car Dyke Roman Canal means that people have occupied the area for a very long time and Saxon pottery and other remains have been unearthed here. There are some interesting houses in the village seen during the walk – the Manor House in the Main Street, Hall Farm in Church Street and the 12th century church of St John the Baptist. The parish has adopted the Countryside Agency's Parish Paths Partnership Scheme (3P's) which means that their public rights of way are maintained by enthusiastic local volunteers. Langtoft, whose church spire is a landmark hereabouts and towards which we walk, belonged in Saxon times to the Abbey of Peterborough and this neighbouring village was burnt by the Danes when they destroyed that town during one of their raids.

The Baskervilles

The Baskervilles is an elegant surprise situated in a village off a main road. Attractive and inviting it has a large central bar and offers seven real ales, including Pedigree, Bass, Tetley, Tiger, John Smith's and Speckled Hen. It also serves draught Scrumpy Jack cider and Guinness. The bar snack menu is extensive, ranging from the usual ploughman's served with a hot, crusty cob to baguettes with various fillings and sandwiches. Main meals include steaks served with salad garnish and vegetable of the day with a choice of chips, spirals, jacket potatoes or rice. Fish, mixed grill, duck breast and pork chops plus a number of vegetarian dishes are also on offer. Serving hours for meals are 12 noon to 2.30 pm and 6 pm to 9.30 pm throughout the week while opening hours are 11 am to 11 pm Monday to Saturday and 12 noon to 2.30 pm and 6 pm to 10.30 pm on Sunday. It is not a free house but belongs to the Tom Hosking Group. Accommodation is available. There is a beer garden and a garden area. Dogs are permitted but only in the bar. Telephone: 01778 560010.

The Walk

① From the pub car park turn back towards the main road and turn left upon reaching the church, with the church on the right. After a few yards, in the road corner where it turns sharply right walk straight forward on a narrow signposted public footpath. Continue straight forward through the Aveland

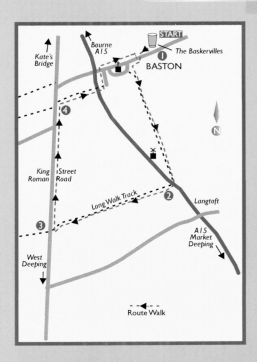

housing development and across the field on a clearly marked path with eventually Hudson's Old Mill over on the right. Continue to the stile and signpost at the A15.

PLACES OF INTEREST NEARBY

Baston Fen is a 90-acre nature reserve. This is the last remnant of true Fenland landscape in Lincolnshire.

Greatford, almost in sight of Baston, is a quiet village centred around the church and private residence Greatford Hall and gardens. Around the village are stone sculptures which were created over a hundred years ago by the former owner of the Hall. Close to the church is the Tithe Barn which is said to be the best example in Lincolnshire. A public footpath leads round from the church.

The Long Walk path to King Street

② Turn left and cross the busy road with care to turn right off the road. Follow the Long Walk for $^3/_4$ mile with the hedge on your right until you reach King Street.

③ Turn right up King Street for 1,300 yards. Some 300 yards after the lane from Greatford comes in on the left, turn right across a small ditchboard onto a signposted footpath. Beware this footbridge for it is often slippy and we have asked for wire to be put over it.

④ Having turned right off King Street the path rapidly improves and it has been nicely landscaped into the new development on the left. Go straight across a main road onto a narrow path by buildings and turn left on arriving at the small road down to Main Street. Turn right along Church Street up to the church where you rejoin your original route from the Baskervilles.

Crowland
The Abbey Hotel

MAP REF: OS EXPLORER 235
(GR 241104)

WALK 29

DISTANCE: $3^3/_4$ MILES

DIRECTIONS TO START: TAKE THE A1073 PETERBOROUGH ROAD SOUTH FROM SPALDING FOR CROWLAND AFTER 10 MILES. THE ABBEY HOTEL IS JUST ACROSS THE ROAD FROM THE ENTRANCE TO CROWLAND ABBEY. **PARKING:** IN THE HOTEL CAR PARK.

The history of this strangely remote little market town has been shaped by water – by river and the fens, which you will appreciate on this enjoyable walk. Only just above fen level today, it was once an island in a vast, swampy countryside. Cru-land meant soft, muddy ground and it was here that St Guthlac landed on a patch of dry ground above the dismal marsh, determined to live a life of hardship and austerity. Ethelbald, the future king of Mercia sought out St Guthlac for spiritual counsel and he later founded the abbey in remembrance of his friend and advisor. Today the north aisle serves as a parish church but splendid fragments of the abbey remain – the ruined nave with its glorious west front, the lovely west arch of the central tower and a portion of the south aisle.

Half a mile from the town by the Spalding road there is a noticeboard about Henry Girdlestone who walked from that spot to an inn in the town for 1,000 hours to complete 1,000 miles. There is no compulsion for you to attempt to rival his feat!

The Abbey Hotel

The Abbey Hotel in East Street is under new ownership and today it is a tastefully restored 17th century coaching house in this historic town. The large old dining room has gone and now the dining area is a pleasant raised section of the main lounge. Drinks on offer are Whitbread's Best Mild, Heineken, Fosters, Stella Artois, Youngers Tavern, John Smith's Cask and Extra Smooth, Strongbow cider and Murphy's Stout plus guest ales. There is also a wide selection of wine. All the food is cooked by a former Joint Services Chef of the Year Finalist. The lunch time menus include sandwiches, toasties, baguettes, omelettes and ploughman's plus soups and stews. There is a morning special of tea or coffee with a set of freshly baked cakes, served with cream or ice cream. The evening meals offer a full range of starters, main courses, sweets, cheese and biscuits and coffee with mints. The opening hours are Monday to Friday 11 am to 3 pm and 6 pm to 11 pm, Saturday 11 am to 11 pm and Sunday 12 noon to 10.30 pm. Meals are available from Monday to Friday 11 am to 2.30 pm and 7 pm to 10 pm, Saturday 11 am to 10 pm, and Sunday 12 noon to 3 pm and 7 pm to 9.30 pm. Telephone: 01733 210200.

The Walk

① Turn left down East Street from the hotel car park with the War Memorial on your right and down to the Trinity

PLACES OF INTEREST NEARBY

Peakirk Waterfowl Gardens, 7 miles north of Peterborough off the A15 at Glinton, are 20 acres of woodland, water, grassy sward and formal gardens, with 135 species of ducks, geese, swans and flamingoes. Telephone: 01733 252271.

Flag Fen Bronze Age Excavations are signposted off the A47 and A1139 2 miles east of Peterborough city centre. A recreated fenland environment and archaeological park with working excavations, reconstructions and primitive farm animals. Telephone: 01733 313414.

Triangular Bridge. The famous Triangular Bridge is a relic unique in the land. Built when the streets were waterways, it is like three halves of bridges meeting in the centre and climbed by three flights of steps. Erected in the second half of the 14th century, it replaced a wooden bridge mentioned in a document 1,000 years ago.

Turn right along North Street and left up the signposted footpath at Wheatsheaf Yard directly opposite the Hollywood kiosk in the middle of the road. Continue forward through the new development to West Bank. Cross the road and climb the embankment to follow the footpath to the right. Turn left on arrival at Riverside but take care to follow the left track.

② After 250 yards turn left along the good track labelled on your map as Middle Road and continue for $1^1/_2$ miles. Turn left at the track junction to the motorable track.

③ By the complex of sluices drop down the track to turn left along Low Road

The famous Triangular Bridge in Crowland

walking towards the abbey or, depending upon the wind and weather, walk along the top of the parallel embankment.

④ At the end of Low Road turn left up the embankment and follow this to the right until you come to where you joined West Bank on the outward walk. There is a public footpath but it only cuts off two houses. Turn right on leaving Wheatsheaf Yard and up East Street to your starting point.

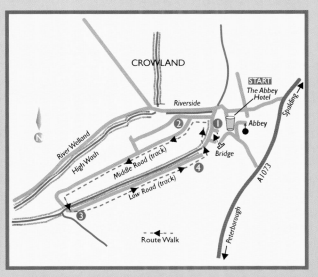

Stamford
The Golden Fleece

| MAP REF: OS EXPLORER 15 (GR 030070) | WALK 30 | DISTANCE: 4½ MILES |

DIRECTIONS TO START: FROM THE A1 NORTH OR SOUTH, TURN OFF FOR STAMFORD.
PARKING: NOT POSSIBLE AT THE GOLDEN FLEECE BUT THE EXTENSIVE BATH ROW
CAR PARK (SIGNPOSTED) ON THE RIVERSIDE IS ONLY YARDS AWAY.

This walk has everything: a well frequented pleasant river meadow, a river bank stroll with items of historical interest en route, a beautiful stone-built village, some woodland walking, entrancing distant views of Stamford's towers and spires, ruins of an ancient hall and downhill all the way after arrival at the Old Great North Road to a welcoming landlord and an interesting inn. Stamford lies in the rich limestone belt in the valley of the Welland and the town is built of local stone. It became wealthy with the wool trade and has three great churches, St Mary's, All Saints and St George's. Later, in the 18th century the increase in traffic on the Great North Road brought another wave of prosperity. However, a reminder of the dangerous past is seen as one enters St Martin's. The welcoming bar across the High Street by the George was once the gallows, mounted as a gesture of warning to highwaymen and dishonest travellers.

The Golden Fleece

The Golden Fleece's name and sign are obviously a reference not only to the legend but also to the sheep market which was held just outside the front door. This friendly traditional pub with a long bar and brass footrails is an Everard's house, a small independent brewery now operating from Castle Acre in Norfolk. Woodpecker cider, Caffrey's Irish Ale, draught Guinness, Stella Artois and Carling Black Label lagers, Tiger Best Bitter, Beacon Bitter, Old Speckled Hen and Old Original are on offer. Hot chocolate and cappuccino coffee are also on sale all day. There is a non-smoking dining room available. Very reasonable bar meals are served from 12 noon to 2.15 pm, including a roast, home-made steak and kidney pie or home-made Lincolnshire sausage pie. The pub is open from 10.30 am to 11 pm from Monday to Saturday and on Sunday from 12 noon to 10.30 pm. Telephone: 01780 763749.

The Walk

① From the Bath Row Car Park, cross the footbridge to walk to the right across The Meadows to the river bank. Look at the information display en route. On reaching the river bank turn right and follow the path. It is called Vence Way to commemorate the twinning of the town with Vence in the south of France. After ¼ mile the path crosses the River Welland and leaves the river to pass through a tunnel below the A1. From there cross a field to a footbridge first over the railway and then a small stream which is the county boundary.

② Walk uphill on a clear path towards the woodland. This path is the route for three long distance recreational paths. On reaching the wood the path has trees on both sides at first and then an open field on the left. Cross two further fields with stiles and waymarks indicating the route and walk straight forward to Easton House (waymark) and through their car park with signpost and Jurassic Way sign. Turn left at Church Lane which is first a track and then a road leading downhill to the attractive stone-built village of Easton on the Hill with some interesting dwellings en route. Turn left at the road junction to walk up to the main road. On reaching the A43 turn left on the footway for 175 yards.

③ Cross the main road with care to follow the signposted public right of way and bridleway to Wothorpe, through the woodland to Wothorpe House. This was built in the early 17th century for Thomas, Earl of Exeter, Lord Burghley's eldest son, who died in 1623. The house was once described as 'the least noble of houses'. It has been in ruins since the 18th century. Do not turn left at the track junction but continue along the bridleway with the ruin on your left. It is just over ½ mile, crossing the A1 on the way and the track becomes the tree-lined Warren

PLACES OF INTEREST NEARBY
Burghley House is open from 11 am to 4.30 pm from April until October. Built on the remains of a 12th century monastery it is now proclaimed as one of the grandest Elizabethan houses in England.

The impressive entrance to Burghley Park

forward along Fryer's Callis and then take the left-hand fork into Wothorpe Road, to the footbridge leading to The Meadows, Bath Row Car Park and the Golden Fleece.

*Alternatively, instead of turning at First Drift continue straight down the road downhill all the way to the traffic lights, passing some interesting buildings on the way. Turn left along Station Road and after 300 yards right leaving another car park and toilets on your left, to the footbridge leading to The Meadows, Bath Row Car Park and the Golden Fleece.

Road, although still only a motorable track, until you reach the Old Great North Road. The long wall on the right when you reach the road is the boundary wall of Burghley Park with its impressive entrance at St Martin's Without.

④ Turn left down the road for 600 yards before turning left along First Drift by the St Martin's Without sign.* After 100 yards take the stile on the right and follow the path down the field edge to a stile in the right-hand field corner, then another stile and a small ditchboard. Continue forward to the kissing gate on the right and then diagonally right across the field to the right-hand field corner to a short track leading to the road. Cross the road and walk straight

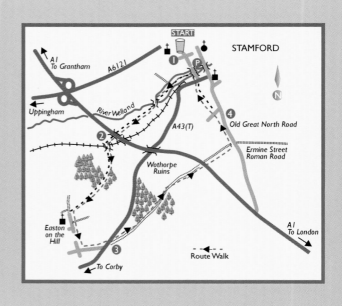